The
Country
Diary
NATURE
NOTES

Small Tortoiseshell
(Vanessa Urticæ)

Meadow Sweet
or
Queen of the Meadow
(Spiræa salicifolia)

Small Upright St John's Wort
(Hypericum pulchrum)

Stinging Nettle
(Urtica Dioica)

NATURE NOTES
OF
THE
COUNTRY DIARY OF
AN EDWARDIAN LADY

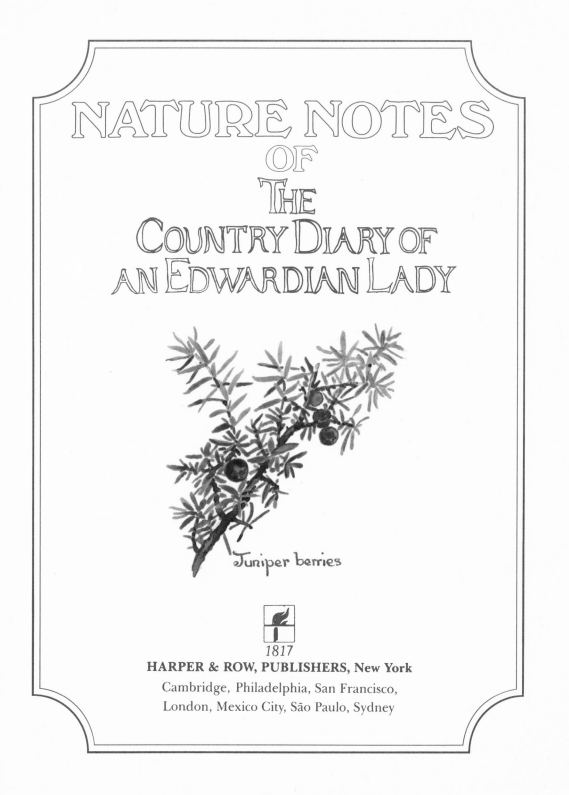

Juniper berries

1817

HARPER & ROW, PUBLISHERS, New York

Cambridge, Philadelphia, San Francisco,
London, Mexico City, São Paulo, Sydney

A *Webb&Bower* Book

Copyright © 1984 Webb & Bower Limited

All rights reserved. Printed in Italy. No part of this book
may be used or reproduced in any manner whatsoever without
written permission except in the case of brief quotations
embodied in critical articles and reviews. For information
address Harper & Row, Publishers, Inc., 10 East 53rd Street,
New York, N.Y. 10022.

FIRST EDITION

Designer: Peter Wrigley

The illustrations and quotations in this book have been
selected from Edith Holden's *The Country Diary of an
Edwardian Lady,* a facsimile reproduction of a naturalist's
diary for the year 1906. Copyright © 1977 Webb & Bower Limited

The publishers would like to thank Rowena Stott, Edith Holden's
great-niece and the owner of the original work, who has made
the publication of this book possible.

Library of Congress Cataloging in Publication Data

Holden, Edith, 1871-1920.
    The country diary nature notes.

    Includes the author's Country diary of an Edwardian
lady, with parallel complementary text by Alan C. Jenkins.
    1. Natural history—England—Warwickshire.
2. Country life—England—Warwickshire. 3. Holden,
Edith, 1871-1920. 4. Illustrators—England—Biography.
I. Jenkins, Alan C. II. Title.
QH138.W37H64 1984   574.9424'97   83-48121

ISBN 0-06-015226-5

83 84 85 86 87 10 9 8 7 6 5 4 3 2 1

John Ray, the seventeenth-century pioneer of modern natural history, remarked in *The Wisdom of God* that 'the treasures of Nature are inexhaustible. If man ought to reflect upon his Creator the glory of all his works, then ought he to take notice of them all and not to think anything unworthy of his cognizance.'

Edith Holden would surely have echoed that sentiment. In every way in *The Country Diary* she shows her delight in all 'great nature's plan', whether frost crystals encrusting the skeletons of plants—a kingfisher flashing along a stream—the dark, disturbing beauty of the viper—the never-failing wonder of a bird's nest—wild roses trailing their garlands over the midsummer hedges. Everything was of interest to her, everything had to be noted down.

Kingfisher

Her entries were brief and simple, some might say unsophisticated. But that is to miss the point. Edith compiled her diary for herself alone. She had no possible idea that one day it would be published and enjoyed across half the world, remote from her Warwickshire byways and streams. She concerned herself with recording the natural sights and sounds and incidents,

Crab·Apple (*Pyrus malus*)

flowers, birds, beasts, insects and weather that caught her eye, and it is this unpretentiousness and freshness that constitutes the diary's appeal. The diary or journal that is self-conscious, playing to some future gallery, becomes artificial and suspect.

Apart from her evident love of nature, Edith shows how pleasurable and valuable a nature diary can be. Indeed, the recording of day-to-day happenings—the changing seasons, the variations in the plumage of birds, their song, their behaviour, the arrival of migrants, the emergence of insects and the burgeoning of wildflowers—is not only a pleasure and a satisfaction, but is essential for anyone at all interested in nature. Nature study (a poor word) without keeping a record of our observations is rather like playing a cricket match without bothering to keep the score.

As Edith knew, every observation must be put down at once, for human memory fades all too quickly, impressions become blurred and accuracy suffers. But the briefest first notes can subsequently be transcribed into something fuller, and gradually be built up into a rich personal journal of nature through the seasons. Year by year a valuable storehouse of natural history will be acquired, to be cherished and enjoyed.

Edith's world was very different from ours. Nearly eighty years ago the countryside was relatively unspoilt. It was the England of Thomas Hardy, W. H. Hudson, Edward Thomas and Flora Thompson. However, even today there is still much scope for the amateur naturalist. Though wildlife is lamentably less abundant, we have compensatory advantages. We enjoy greater mobility, enabling us, for example, to go and watch grey seals on the western rocks, to make bird-watching tours round the coasts of Britain and to visit the haunts of avocet and osprey. Guided nature trails, mini-safaris even, abound and ornithological groups sally forth every weekend—though it has to be interpolated here that human numbers and nature-watching aren't always compatible. To quote John Ray again, 'the stars were not made just to twinkle at us'. Nature exists not simply for our benefit; many a rare plant has been collected to extinction, many a bird, rare or otherwise, deserts its nest because of too much human curiosity. For example, the RSPB's devoted guardianship of Red kites in north Wales is as much to protect them against over-enthusiastic 'twitchers' as against egg-thieves. The best and most satisfying nature study is done by the solitary individual.

But to revert: there are nowadays all manner of easily available aids for the nature-lover—microscopes for the entomologist—bird-recordings (bird-song is a vital means of identification, for many birds are heard rather than seen)—tape-recorders—powerful binoculars—lightning-fast cameras, contrasting strikingly with those cumbersome plate affairs pioneers such as Richard and Cherry Kearton had to lug around.

And on all sides there are means of increasing our knowledge of nature, brilliant television films, expert classes and lectures, innumerable guide-books covering every subject—bird-identification, animal-tracks, photography, flora, fungi, sea-shore, pond and river. There is the opportunity to visit natural sanctuaries such as the Wildfowl Trust's Slimbridge and many of the RSPB's and the Nature Conservancy's reserves. In addition to all this there exist many societies, both national and local, of help and interest to the amateur ornithologist or botanist or entomologist.

In the end, the essentials of nature-watching or nature study are infinite patience, a willingness to endure discomfort at times, and the underlying wish to look, even in a limited way, into the world of nature. But there is no need to start off too ambitiously and risk being disappointed. In many cases nature is on our doorstep. In these days of the urban fox, the local park or common will often produce unexpected creatures, the local canal, the abandoned quarry can teem with a variety of life of all kinds; even the derelict graveyard will be found to have its own inhabitants, plant and animal.

The nature notes in this book are not intended as a practical guide. They seek to elaborate on some of the items chronicled in Edith Holden's diary, to encourage, it is hoped, people to keep their own nature diaries or journals, and to stimulate awareness of the nature that still exists around us, while showing too that there is pleasure and interest to be found in the apparently most insignificant wildlife.

January

Blue Tits

Cole Tit
Great Tit

JANUARY

New Year's Day. Bright and cold with hard
frost.

Great gale of wind and rain from the south-west.

1

2

3

4

5

6

7

JANUARY

It is fitting in a book such as *The Country Diary* that already, amid the frost and gales in January, there should be signs of hope in the form of the leaf-buds of the elder showing green and the wild arum thrusting up its distinctive sheath, looking like a tightly-rolled umbrella. Both are interesting plants for different reasons. It's often surprising to find quite low-growing elders flourishing round rabbit warrens—though it has to be said that since myxomatosis really numerous rabbit colonies are a rarer occurrence. But the elder is one of the few plants those inveterate nibblers don't eat. Many a gardener must wish his produce was similarly uninviting.

As for the wild arum—alias cuckoo-pint, lords-and-ladies, the devil's men and women, not forgetting wake-robin—its name brings to mind Carl Linnaeus, the great eighteenth-century naturalist. He was the pioneer of the modern system of nomenclature, before his time scientific names having been as cumbersome as a sledge-hammer, enough to crush any flower. In his condemnation of what he called 'this appalling diagnosis', he instanced the arum, then known as *Arum summis labris degustantes mutos reddens*, which, being rendered into English, if it can be so termed, meant the Arum-which-strikes-dumb-those-who-do-but-taste-it. Linnaeus rationalized it into *Arum maculatum* or spotted arum.

Now, a rose by any other name may smell as sweet, but it greatly enhances the pleasure to be able to distinguish between different species, particularly if you are keeping a nature journal or diary. Edith Holden, a true botanist, knew this well enough, and she carefully lists both the popular and scientific names of species.

The moorhen, correctly the water-hen, she mentions and illustrates is interesting, too, for very different reasons. Totally unrelated, it puts one in mind of the hoatzin of faraway South America because of one of its attributes. Though in a much less pronounced way, the sooty-black baby water-hen possesses on its 'bastard' wing a distinct nail or claw which it can use for climbing, when it wants to get back into the nest, which it will attempt to do several times if necessary. And the adult water-hen has a strange, unexplained habit of flying at night. It will do this even in built-up areas, flying between houses, but sometimes coming to grief by colliding with overhead wires—which explains the occasional discovery of a dead bird far from its habitual pond.

JANUARY

Today I saw a curious Oak-tree, growing in a field near Elmdon Park. From a distance it look- ed as if half of the tree were dead and the other half covered with glossy green leaves.

8

9

10

11

12

13

14

Though this pretty, neat bird, with its graceful action, often skulks unseen among the sedges and willows of the water's edge, its presence made known by its loud metallic call, it isn't really timid and will even mingle with farmyard poultry and share their food—an opportunity increasingly rare. But among its fellows it can be exceedingly aggressive. Male rivals will often fight fiercely on land or water for territory or a mate. They use their long splayed feet (the toes of which are slightly flanged for walking on lily-pads and other floating plants) like game-cocks.

Edith's reaction to 'a curious Oak-tree' which looked as if half of it were dead and the other covered in glossy leaves is typical of the good nature-watcher, in whom curiosity is an essential virtue. Though the tree stands at a considerable distance she goes out of her way to investigate, finding that the illusion has been caused by two different species growing together in close embrace. One is a 'conventional' oak, the other an evergreen or holm-oak or turkey-oak. This sort of natural partnership is of course quite fortuitous and is sometimes found with other trees such as holly and hawthorn intertwined with similar curious effect. It is quite different from the parasitical activities of, say, the ivy which wraps itself round many a tree.

Altogether, world-wide, there are some three hundred species of oak. The two main types in Britain are the pendunculate oak, recognizable by its stalked acorns and elaborately shaped leaves, and the durmast or sessile oak whose acorns have no stalks and whose leaf-blades have starlike hairs on their under-surface. The oak is one of our vanished or vanishing glories. Once upon a time much of southern England was majestically garbed in oak-woods. They were variously felled for land clearance, industrial use, and for that other erstwhile pride, the navy.

Edith, as any lover of nature must, always took note of the weather, for this is an essential part of the natural scene—the backdrop, as it were. She never failed to respond to any particularly beautiful aspect, as in the instance where she describes the effect of the frost and its superb, intricate crystals. The phenomenon variously known as the Ammil (a term used in Devonshire, which she visited from time to time) or silver-thaw occurs when, in rapid succession, snow and

JANUARY

The green leaves are out on the Woodbine too making little spots of green among the under--growth.

15

16

17

18

19

20

21

frost, thaw and humidity in the form of fog or rain, followed again by a frost that glazes everything, combine to produce a dramatic and ravishing effect, so that the countryside resembles an illustration from Hans Andersen or Topelius.

One of the most striking features of this is the speed with which it happens if the atmospheric conditions are right. As if at the touch of a wand, every single object from gorse-bush to dead seed-vessel, every twig and branch and fence and stone, even the forgotten skull of a rabbit, becomes glazed over in dazzling beauty unmatched by any craftsman in porcelain. A detailed record of the weather is an important part of any nature journal—and in this respect an amusing sideline is to collect as many country weather sayings as possible and test their reliability.

It almost goes without saying that the gorse is in flower even in inclement January—some of it at least. That's one old country saying which is completely accurate—'when kissing is out of favour, gorse is out of bloom', for it is a fact that *some* flowers of the gorse or whin can be seen at any time of year, whether it is Easter or Midsummer or Christmas. But its greatest burnished glory comes in April and May when the massed flowers, responding to the midday sun, give forth a subtle fragrance which W. H. Hudson likened to some strange dreamlike heavenly heady incense.

The woodbine, which Edith mentions flecking the undergrowth with green—and you've got to look down as well as up and on all sides in nature—is usually an alias for the honeysuckle, as in *A Midsummer Night's Dream*. But in fact in the past, 'woodbine' was applied to almost any creeping or climbing plant, even the wild clematis and the convolvulus, and, in America, the Virginia creeper.

We tend to think of bird migration in terms of swallows and swifts and warblers from Africa and wild geese and wading birds from the Arctic. But those large flocks of rooks and starlings Edith noted foraging ·on the fields may well have comprised winter migrants from the Continent. A single instance—ten thousand migrant starlings have been counted in a space of two hours flying over the Kent coast. Similarly, large numbers of rooks fly in from Germany and Scandinavia and even Russia. Maybe collective farm-workers round Smolensk or Minsk sometimes look up from their spring sowing later on and welcome back their rooks as a sign of the changing season!

JANUARY

Primroses, Polyanthus, Winter Aconite, Mazereon and Snowdrops are all in flower in the garden. Every mild morning now the birds are singing and they continue more or less throughout the day.

22

23

24

25

26

27

28

JANUARY

The unusual silvery-grey, almost white robin mentioned in *The Country Diary* is a colour variation liable to occur in all species, though it seems to be more common in some. Completely white house-sparrows occur from time to time, while blackbirds splashed in a haphazard fashion with blotches of white, as if the target of some random paintbrush, are by no means uncommon. This is due to a lack of chemical pigment, the chief source of colour in birds, which is carried to the feathers in the bloodstream through the opening in the base of the quills. But some colour is caused by the refraction of light on the microscopic structure of the feathers.

However, the silvery-white robin or the 'pied' blackbird are not true albinos, unlike white mice and certain kinds of white rabbit, whose eyes are of a pinkish colour. Conversely, as well as the lack of the right pigment which produces albinism, there is the phenomenon of melanism caused by an excess of black pigment which produces exceptionally dark colouring and is seen occasionally in pheasants.

Edith faithfully reflects the charmingly abrupt switches that take place in the English climate. One moment biting frost makes you blow your finger-nails or shrouding fog disorientates the birds; next there is a chaplet of flowers to be noted and painted, not only primrose and polyanthus and winter aconite that brighten the garden, but the humbler yet no less welcome daisy—beloved of the poet Chaucer, who said that the mere blissful sight of it each morning softened his sorrow—and that even humbler 'weed', the groundsel, which can be seen in flower all the year round and whose seeds are enjoyed so much by the goldfinch.

Altogether in her diary, Edith mentions well over two hundred wildflowers, and as she lived so close to Stratford, it is not inapposite to remark that in his plays Shakespeare mentioned one hundred and seventy varieties, both garden and wild. Some of the flowers that feature in *The Country Diary*, Shakespeare never knew or never mentioned. Neither the foxglove, surprisingly, nor the forget-me-not, nor even the delicately defiant snowdrop find a place in his lines. Perhaps not so surprisingly with the snowdrop, for it is not a native of Britain, being considered an escapee from some monastery garden, so maybe it had not yet spread so widely in his days.

JANUARY

Saw several Moorhens feeding on a newly
ploughed fields, not far from a pond.

The last few weeks, our own and our neighbours'
gardens have been haunted by a very curious Robin

29

30

31

NOTES

February

FEBRUARY

Snow-storm in the night, this morning we looked out on a white landscape, this is the first deep snow we have had this winter. I swept a space free on the lawn and strewed it with bread and rice: Crowds of birds came.

1

2

3

4

5

6

7

Dog's Mercury
(Mercurialis perennis)

=FEBRUARY=

One old country saw about the weather doesn't seem to be borne out by *The Country Diary*. Now, according to an old Yorkshire saying, if Candlemas Day (2 February) is calm and fair, half the winter is still to come. Whereas if it is murky and foul, as it is in Edith's February, then the worst of the winter is already over. But this is disproved because it is immediately followed by rain, hail, sleet, and deepening snow!

And of course long before the traditional St Valentine's Day, there are always over-enthusiastic birds that are caught out by the weather, their early nests filled with snow, their food supplies diminished at a crucial time. But in their urgent need to perpetuate their species, birds start to quarrel and mate while winter is still in full sway, stimulated as much by the growing light as the temperature. Rooks, as we see here, regularly visit their nests during winter, putting in a stint of repair-work and solemnly discussing the prospects. Ravens are perhaps the earliest of nesters, rivalled by the assertive mistle-thrush which has the unfortunate habit of sitting conspicuously on some exposed branch with an astonishingly large bundle of nesting-material in its beak, while it builds its nest in an equally conspicuous position for any marauding magpie to observe.

Some species, notably the house-sparrow and the ring-dove, scarcely let up in their domestic activities. Eggs of both these prolific species have often been found in midwinter.

It is in weather such as Edith mentions that feeding birds is of immense value. In really severe times not only does it often make the difference between life and death but it also brings unusual species to the garden to partake of the bounty, even normally shy birds such as redwings which, in spite of coming from a subarctic habitat, are very susceptible to cold. In really epic winters even partridges have been recorded as visiting homesteads.

For many generations people have fed the wild birds, but the now familiar bird-table has a relatively short history. When the late Hugh Massingham wrote his *Sanctuaries for Birds and How to make them* sixty years ago, the bird-table was still a novelty. The bird-table, which anyone can construct, without depending on the elaborate articles constantly advertised, is an admirable starting-point for bird-watching—identifying species, observing their different characteristics and behaviour. Even among species there is a marked

FEBRUARY

It says in today's Chronicle that at Dover a Blackbird's nest with two eggs has been found. at Edenbridge a Hedge-sparrow's with four eggs and at Elmstead, a robin's with five eggs.

8

9

10

11

12

13

14

Dog's Mercury
(Mercurialis perennis)

individuality in birds and as distinct a pecking order as in domestic poultry. There's amusement, too, in seeing how birds can be said literally to snarl at each other, opening their beaks aggressively and trying to outface each other.

In this respect one of the most pugnacious is the mercurial blue-tit—bluecap, as Edith calls it. With its brilliant cerulean blues and handsome yellows, it is a fizzing, bouncing scrap of a bird, aggressive out of all proportion to its size. I have seen it grapple fiercely with a nuthatch, twice its size, both birds falling locked in combat from the table to continue fighting on the ground.

And the bird-table may well provide an opportunity to disprove the slander traditionally levelled at the sparrow for killing cock-robin. It is much more likely to be the robin who indulges in truly mortal combat, being one of the few birds which will actually commit murder among its fellows. (Does this explain its remarkable affinity with Man?)

But although a bird-table provides great pleasure for the householder, especially if a regular notebook is kept, nesting-boxes, too, can be of value to many birds, for habitat-space is of paramount importance to them. It should be said that different species need different help in this way. Not all birds will take readily to what you devotedly put up for them. In this connection the British Trust for Ornithology has published a useful 'Field Guide' on the subject.

Nest and eggs
   of Blackbird.

FEBRUARY

Walking home from Solihull this afternoon I noticed
a number of Gnats dancing in the bright sunshine.
and I saw two little Shrew-Mice in different places
on the bank, who darted quickly into their holes directly
they saw me.

15

16

17

18

19

20

21

Dog's Mercury
(Mercurialis perennis)

=FEBRUARY=

One of the most pleasant, if not always comprehensible sights in winter, as *The Country Diary* records, is a crowd of gnats dancing interminably in the glittering air, often under the branches of some towering oak—a nice contrast that illustrates the marvellously varied scale of nature: the huge, noble tree that has been several centuries a-growing and the tiny, ephemeral creatures whose life-span is measured in hours, days at most—and whose larvae, incidentally, may well be living in the decaying leaves of that same oak.

Although these dancing hordes are known as winter gnats, they can in fact be found all the year round, the commonest species being *Trichocera annulata*. Another member of the order of Diptera may make its presence known at this time of year in a rather different way. This is *Theobaldia annulata*, a large mosquito identifiable by the white rings on its legs and body. You may not see it, but you will be aware of its quite sharp bite, for it often rouses up temporarily in any warm spell in winter.

Other more likeable insects to be seen occasionally during a sunny spell are a few honey-bees. But they aren't out on a vain search for blossom. They are individual bees partaking in a cleansing flight. The worker bee is the epitome of cleanliness, scrupulously removing any droppings from the hive, while if any intruder, such as a snail, dies on the spot and is too heavy to remove, it is mummified by the bees in a shroud of resinous glue.

But this obsession with cleanliness can have fatal consequences for the bees if the weather changes and they become chilled while out on their hygienic rounds.

Edith knew that it is essential for the nature-watcher to keep still, endlessly if necessary, even in discomfort, and even sometimes fruitlessly. But often the reward comes when miniscule life ventures into view, like the shrews she watched one afternoon (they aren't mice, not even rodents: they belong to the order Insectivora). The common shrew, a strange little long-nosed creature, can as often be heard uttering its shrill, irritable twittering cries as actually seen. Edith remarks on the number of shrew corpses frequently to be seen and there may be more than one reason for this.

Small though it is, the shrew can succumb rapidly to starvation, its

FEBRUARY

I gathered some Gorse blossom on my way home.
The Elm trees are just breaking into blossom, and the Willows
are showing their downy white catkins, — very small as yet.

22

23

24

25

26

27

28

Dog's Mercury
(Mercurialis perennis)

metabolism demanding constant food. In addition it is very susceptible to shock. And lastly, though various predators will kill the shrew, they will not necessarily eat it, for it is possessed of a musky flavour not relished by all birds and mammals, though grass-snake and viper will take it.

Shrews in general have always had an evil reputation in folklore, being accused especially of causing cattle-murrain. The shrew-ash was a common phenomenon in mediaeval times, a live shrew being sealed up in a hole in the trunk of an ash tree, to the accompaniment of suitable incantations, a branch of the ash being thereafter endowed with healing qualities if applied to a sick cow or horse. Writing in the early 1600s, Edward Topsell described the shrew as 'a ravening beast, feigning itself gentle or tame, but being touched, it biteth deep, and poisoneth deadly'.

Modern research has proved that to be no old wives' tale, at least not totally, for shrews do indeed possess a toxic secretion in their salivary glands, capable of paralyzing worms and snails. Indeed, applied in sufficient quantity the poison has been shown to be potent enough to kill a mouse.

As Edith says, one of the shrew's chief predators is the weasel, that slim, nimble, supremely neat little hunter of the woods and ditches. Usually it is seen by chance, scurrying across road or track—or, again, as a result of patient watching, a passive activity that never fails to bring some result, for there is always something going on in nature.

It might be said that in the case of the weasel, and also the larger stoat, one's chances of a sighting are often increased by the fact that it is incorrigibly curious and will often come back for another look.

FEBRUARY

The Erd Shrew or Shrew-Mouse, inhabits sub-
terranean tunnels, which it excavates in the
soil. It feeds upon insects and worms; and
it's long, flexible nose is a great aid to it

29

NOTES

Dog's Mercury
(Mercurialis perennis)

March

MARCH

March has come in like a lamb with a warm wind and rain from the South-west.

Glorious sunshine. First warm day of Spring. All the Sky-larks up and singing in the blue. Went for a long walk.

1

2

3

4

5

6

7

Daffodils
(Narcissus pseudo-narcissus)

As *The Country Diary* shows so vividly, March truly is the month when nature stirs, when the earth, as it were, rolls over in its sleep after the numbing days of winter. Though we have chafed at some of the rigours of the past months, it is good to remember that during those bleak times the earth has been resting, nature renewing herself, as we do with sleep—though in her case not for a brief night at a time but for weeks on end.

There are many signs of this awakening that Edith noted and painted. One, alas, is scarcely to be seen any more, particularly in the countryside she knew: the blossom of the elm. She would be saddened by the devastation wrought on that noble tree by Dutch Elm disease. The fungus causing this is carried around by a bark-beetle and gets into the tree's 'blood-vessels', choking the tree to death, as we might put it. The farther north, the more chance of the elm surviving, for a good hard winter is the best antidote to the disease. But in many regions it has utterly changed the English landscape of which the elm was once so redolent. Disease and intensive farming have much to answer for!

However, another of Edith's favourite signs of spring is still abundant—the lesser celandine with its glowing, almost waxy yellow flowers. Suddenly, as if at the touch of a switch, in any burst of sunshine, the celandine lights up grassy banks like tiny shards of that same sun—which moved Edward Thomas to remark how the sun on the celandines was redoubled.

The celandine is an interesting plant, for usually it first shows itself when no insects are abroad to help its pollination. Nature, as usual, has an answer for this, having equipped the lesser celandine, alias pilewort, with bulbils, tiny bulblike growths between leaves and stem. In due course these drop off and become new plants.

That toad Edith mentions 'jumping about the hall' is typical of the enthusiasm evinced by all the amphibians with the first clement days of March. Toads and frogs alike, they awake from hibernation full of zest for the renewal of life and their thoughts turn at once to wooing. But occasionally, if a cold spell all at once returns, perhaps with the proverbial blackthorn winter, their spawn may be frozen—if marauding crows or herons haven't dragged it out already. Toads are very prudent in their habits, always returning to their regular breeding-haunts, sometimes at long distances, whereas frogs are

MARCH

Tonight a Toad was discovered jumping about in the hall; it must have come in through the garden door which has been standing open all day. Another day of bright sunshine. The leaf-buds in the hedges have been making wonderful progress these last three days of sunshine and the Elm blossom has opened out wide, showing all its little anthers and filaments.

8

9

10

11

12

13

14

Daffodils
(Narcissus pseudo-narcissus)

much more slap-happy, breeding almost anywhere, even at times in puddles which may subsequently dry up, leaving the spawn to perish. The numbers of both these animals have declined lamentably: anyone who gives them protection will not only be doing them a good turn but will obtain great help in the garden.

Normally the toad doesn't 'jump', but crawls ponderously about his affairs, whereas the frog does hop, in a very sprightly way. The two can best be distinguished by the difference in their skins. The frog's is smooth, moist, even clammy, but certainly not slimy, and is of a yellowish ground colour streaked and spotted with brown. The toad's is dry, warty, generally rough, its colour commonly grey. When Shakespeare spoke of the precious jewel the toad wears in its head he was clearly referring to its bright, coppery eyes.

Many birds make up for their lack of song by their brilliant plumage—like that jay with its pert crest, its vinaceous, almost pink colouring, and its striking wing-patches splendidly barred with blue, black and white. The contrast in this respect is most marked in tropical birds which are often breathtakingly beautiful but by and large lack any song. In comparison, many English birds are soberly clad but their songs are among nature's greatest charms—the passionate outpourings of the song-thrush—the mellow complacency of the blackbird—the rollicking catch of the chaffinch —the shivering cadence of the wood-warbler that has been likened to golden rain. The yellow-hammer would seem to bear all this out: realizing he has no real song, he sits on top of the hedgerow showing off his truly handsome colouring in the sunshine.

As for the skylark, it is surely an even more romantic singer than the nightingale, rising higher and higher on quivering wings, letting fall 'the silver chain of sound, of many links without a break', which can be heard long after the bird has been lost to sight. Singing birds often 'defy' the weather (and what could be a more delightful image than Edith's skylark singing in the midst of the swirling snow-flakes), notably the mistle-thrush, sturdily erect at the top of a tree, flinging, it seems, a challenge to the winter, and well is he nicknamed the storm-cock.

Birds' nests, as Edith shows, never cease to astonish and delight because of the amount of labour and skill—and devotion—involved

MARCH

A beautiful Jay in all the glory of his spring plumage flew screaming across the lane into a spinney of larch trees opposite.

15

16

17

18

19

20

21

Daffodils
(Narcissus pseudo-narcissus)

in building them. Some birds will bravely sit tight in the face of blatant human curiosity, but too much of this may cause desertion. The nature-lover should always resist the temptation to probe too deeply into nature's private life. The old warning that trespassers will be prosecuted should be altered to 'twitchers will be prosecuted'!

One bird in particular has long been active making nests, not just one but several. This is the *male* wren, that nut-brown, stumpy-tailed bullet of a bird, whose song is incredibly explosive for such a feathered mite. He is a compulsive nest-maker—domed nests that will never be used. These are known as cock-nests and are built just anywhere—in haystack—tree-stump—cabbage-head—and once even in the carcass of a sparrowhawk strung up on a branch. Many of these are not finished, but when in March the wren finally makes the ideal home, he leads his mate to it, with much ceremony, for her demure but critical approval.

Wildflowers are ever present in *The Country Diary*—periwinkles, violets, primroses, daffodils, and all those many others that spring up secretly to delight us. At first we count them like trophies, until they become too numerous, but we will prolong the pleasure they give us if we note them down each time. One flower that is mentioned and illustrated runs the risk of being overlooked because of its modest appearance. This is the moschatel, which has a charm of form and tint that will reward the searching eye among the woods and on the banks, where it is often a companion of the gayer celandine. Significantly, its name derives from the Greek meaning 'without glory'. But its pale green flowers, forming a little cluster at the top of the stem, are subtly beautiful, and have a faint, musky scent.

The word catkin is nicely evocative, suggesting something small and endearing. It is said to come from the Dutch 'katteken', a little cat! This is quite fitting, as catkins are always a delightful, welcome phenomenon of nature, delicately adorning hazel and poplar and birch and alder. Many catkin-bearing plants are pollinated by the wind, and sometimes you can see the pollen dust drifting in the air. But the willow, for example, depends on insects to help it.

The caddis grubs Edith features are the larvae of caddis flies, of which in Britain more than one hundred and seventy species exist. It is as grubs or 'worms' that they are probably better known than

MARCH

This morning I saw some Frog-spawn which had been brought in from a pond, together with some Caddis grubs in their funny little cases of sticks and straws. One grub looked very smart, he had stuck his house all over with bits of bright green rush and water plant.

22

23

24

25

26

27

28

Daffodils
(Narcissus pseudo-narcissus)

when in their perfect state. As flies they look rather like small moths and fold their wings over their bodies like a roof. It is in their larval state that they are most interesting. Surrounded by a jelly-like substance, the eggs are laid on the edge of pond or shallow stream, the action of the water gradually dissolving the jelly so that the eggs separate.

Now, the caddis grub has a hard head and thorax, but the rest of its body is soft and vulnerable. So, in order to protect itself, the grub makes an admirable little container, picking up pieces of sticks and leaves, grains of sand, fragments of freshwater shells, fastening them together by means of a fine silk thread which is also used to line the case. With its head sticking out freely, the grub holds the case on by dint of claws at the base of its abdomen. In clear water you can occasionally see caddis cases jerking here and there over the bottom as the grub goes about its minute affairs.

Now particularly is it time for the arrival of the summer bird-migrants, those valiant travellers who come to us from thousands of miles away. Competing, as we might say, to be first, are the wheatear and the chiff-chaff. In a very mild winter a few chiff-chaffs will linger on in the tolerable climate of the south-west and in Ireland. But for most of us, the first indication of the bird's presence is that thrilling *chiff-chiff-chiff* (it's not *chiff-chaffs*) as the bird skulks for shelter if the winds of March are too robust. That welcome call, it should be said, can be confused with the distant note of the great tit, giving rise to some wishful thinking at times.

As for the wheatear, that plump and handsome bird of the moors and downs, he can be recognized instantly—and it's always the male which arrives first—by his smart white rump as he bobs on stone wall or granite rock, crying *chack-chack* repeatedly, as if to say 'Back! I'm back!' Shepherds on the Sussex downs years ago used to catch large numbers of wheatears and sell them to restaurants for their gourmet customers.

The wheatear didn't visit Edith's part of the country, but she saw many other 'sweet birds as I spun along between the hedges', as she says in that splendidly evocative phrase which sums up the pleasure of cycling as a means of seeing the countryside. And from such expeditions she brought back many treasures of nature to transmute through her brush and her pen.

MARCH

Gathered some of the young crimson catkins of the
Black Poplar. The last few days have been very cold
and dry, with keen north wind, and any quantity
of March dust in evidence.

29

30

31

NOTES

Daffodils
(Narcissus pseudo-narcissus)

APRIL

" When daisies red and violet's blue,   And cuckoo-buds of yellow hue,
  And ladie's Smocks' all silver white   Do paint the meadows with delight.'

APRIL

Very still, grey day. I went to a little spinney to see a large bush of the Great Round-leaved Willow, which is a perfect picture just now, covered all over with great golden catkins, that light up the copse like hundreds of little fairy lamps. The bees were humming all round it, busy gathering the pollen.

1

2

3

4

5

6

7

Wood Anemone or Wind-flower
(Anemone nemorosa)

The year is gathering pace. A transformation scene is in progress, 'when', as Shakespeare had it, 'well-apparelled April on the heel of limping winter treads'. And, as Edith proceeds to show us, the month is a treasure-house of natural beauty and happenings and arrivals, so that it seems as if Nature can't wait to spread all her contents before us.

Pace Chaucer, 'the young sun his half-course in the sign of the Ram has run', and the bees are taking advantage of the subsequent warmth—not now merely for cleansing flights, but to fill their pollen-baskets, those marvellous hollowed out little containers on the outer side of their hind legs. But other bees are active too, especially the bumble-bee, of which there are several kinds. The most familiar is *Bombus terrestris*, plump, furry, and decorated with two handsome yellow bands. Any bumble or humble bee observed now will be a queen. For the bumble-bee has a rather sad life cycle—like so many other insects.

The queen has spent the winter hibernating in some snuggery such as a tree-stump. On emerging from her winter sleep, she sets about finding a suitable nursery, preferably the old nest of a field-vole or wood-mouse. Eventually, when there is enough blossom, she makes a cache of honey and pollen in the nest and then lays her eggs (which she has carried all winter), so that on hatching out the young insects have a supply of food to hand.

The worker bumble-bees are considerably smaller than their queen, and during their minute life are ceaselessly engaged in enlarging the nest and gathering nectar and pollen for the increasing number of young bumble-bees bred by the queen. Posterity is their only reward, for with the approach of colder weather all the males and workers die. Only the newly impregnated queens survive to start the cycle afresh.

Far more prominent now (and it could have been seen in March) is the brimstone butterfly which Edith paints. The male especially, with his striking wings, a central orangey-red spot on each one, never fails to thrill us as he flits gaudily through the sunlit air. Greenish-white, the female is less noticeable and usually puts in an appearance later. These brimstones will have emerged from their chrysalides during the previous July or August, and gone into hibernation in due course, often among clumps of ivy leaves, which, themselves turning yellow,

APRIL

Saw the first Swallow and a Yellow Brimstone Butterfly.
Easter Sunday. Another brilliant day. Saw a pair of House Martins,
watched some Trout in the Leet and found a Chaffinch's nest nearly
finished in a young Hawthorn.

8

9

10

11

12

13

14

Wood Anemone or Wind-flower
   (Anemone membrosa)

provide a handy disguise. The brimstone is by far the longest lived of any butterfly and will still be active in the coming July. It is often said that the word butterfly was first applied to the brimstone, this truly 'butter-coloured fly'

Wall butterfly and peacock and garden white have all hibernated, but the painted lady featured in *The Country Diary* must have been a very early migrant, for the species doesn't hibernate here. Its home is in northern Africa, sometimes as far away as Ethiopia, and it is an exceptionally strong flyer, as well it might be to travel such enormous distances on such frail wings. It is also, incidentally, a very late flyer, lingering on in the evening long after other butterflies have gone to rest. Its migrations, in some years particularly noticeable, are probably due to a periodical explosion in its numbers, forcing the butterflies in huge swarms to seek sustenance farther and farther afield. There are few countries in the world that the painted lady doesn't visit, going even as far north as Iceland.

Edith makes a visit to Dartmoor, and there could be no greater contrast with her own lush countryside in the heartland of England, heavy with blossom and flanked on all sides with flowers. But this stark, lonely rocky desert, with its many reminders of its volcanic past, and its remnants of our Bronze Age ancestors, clearly intrigued her—as it does the thousands of visitors that flock to it every year.

The ponies she talks of are not truly wild, except in essence. All are owned, even though their owners scarcely set eyes on them from one year's end to another and most of the stallions and mares have never felt human legs astride them. They live out all the year round, scratching a living from the scrawny pasture, struggling against often fearsome conditions, their manes tassled with frost. Many provide a meal for the barking ravens and mewing buzzards and rock-dwelling foxes ever on watch for a moorland tragedy.

The true-bred Dartmoor pony is an admirably sturdy animal, bay, black or brown in colour, which in proportion to its size, can probably carry a heavier weight than any other breed while at the same time making its way fast and expertly across rough terrain. Its pedigree is zealously guarded, but too often hybrid ponies of the circus type have spoilt the stock. In Edith's day, and right up to the last war, spectacular 'drifts' used to take place when hundreds of

APRIL

Bright and cold. Saw two live Vipers which had been brought
in from the moor; one of them was more than two feet
long. The gentleman who had captured them handled
them quite fearlessly, he held one up by the back of the
neck and forcing it's mouth open with a stick, he showed me
the two little pink fangs in the upper jaw.

15

16

17

18

19

20

21

Wood Anemone or Wind-flower
(Anemone membrosa)

ponies would be rounded up and taken to a huge central pound. The drift calls to mind a cattle-drive on some western prairie, the different droves or herds coming in from all quarters at the headlong speed unbroken ponies can keep up for miles on end—all of which called for supremely skilful riding by the moormen rounding them up.

An encounter of a different kind recorded by Edith was with the vipers of Dartmoor. They are still common enough and are as likely to be seen now as they emerge in the warm spring sunshine and slough their skins—which they will do three or four times through the year. The viper or adder is a much maligned creature, not nearly as desperate a character as suggested in the Reverend J. G. Wood's *Natural History*, quoted by Edith. During the present century only a dozen deaths have resulted from snake-bite in this country, the viper being a peace-loving animal only too willing to get out of the way.

There shouldn't be any difficulty in distinguishing between the viper and the harmless grass-snake. Generally speaking, the viper is dark coloured—it can be quite black—and usually has a zig-zag stripe along its back. Its jaws are more prominent, the head shows up more distinctively, whereas with the grass-snake there's an absence of a defined neck. In colour the grass-snake is usually an olive-green with an unmistakable yellow patch on either side of the neck; the pupil of its eye is round, not slit-like as in the viper. And the grass-snake is much longer and more graceful than the thickset viper—which, in the female, the larger of the sexes, rarely reaches more than two and a quarter feet in length, whereas the female grass-snake has been known to exceed four feet.

Burrator reservoir which Edith visited while on Dartmoor had only recently been built—the dam was completed in 1898. So she would not have been able to appreciate how singularly beautiful it has become, with its attendant phalanxes of coniferous and deciduous woodlands and its neighbouring bosky gulleys.

But there was plenty to catch her eye: a heron winging its steady way across the artificial lake—for it doesn't take nature long to exploit any new habitat: tadpoles going through that perilous process of turning into miniature frogs: a kestrel hovering in supreme mastery of the air: a leveret crouching until the last moment in its 'form' in the hope of being passed by unseen. Unfortunately, since

APRIL

Bright sun and strong North east wind. Set out for a walk to Lowry.
Going over Yannadon Down we saw a young Hare lying in it's form
among the gorse bushes. It lay quite still till we had all but trodden
on it, when it dashed off among the heather and gorse.
Going down the long, steep lane to Lowry, we found some pink
Milk-wort, Tormentil and Germander Speedwell in flower on
the bank.

22

23

24

25

26

27

28

Wood Anemone or Wind-flower
(Anemone membrosa)

Edith's day, the once common hare, almost a pest in some areas, has now become far less numerous, partly owing to intensive agricultural methods. Cobbett's famous 'acre of hares' will never be seen again.

However, it is always to the wildflowers that we return and Edith has the happy knack of opening our eyes to all the floral galaxy that stars the earth. For her it is a case of 'the constellated flower that never sets'.

For some people botany is a daunting subject, bringing to mind the odious Mr Squeers—'when he has learnt that bottiney means a knowledge of plants, he goes and gets 'em. That's our system.' But there is no lack of worthy guides to the subject, a knowledge of which will enrich anyone's enjoyment of nature. Not only will the name of flower or shrub or tree add to the interest and pleasure, as we suggested earlier, but so also will a knowledge of how the flower is reproduced. For in most cases its reproduction is a wonderful example of nature's interaction. The flower produces nectar to attract the insects—not only the honey-bees and butterflies, but hover-flies and bluebottles and so many others—which, in helping themselves to the nectar at the bases of the petals or pollen from the stamens, carry this to other flowers in a never-ending process.

Besides, botany can be pursued at home—in the garden—along the footpath—on the neighbouring common—far more readily than some other nature studies. Flowers stay put, they don't flash off into cover or dart into their burrow when you approach.

Additionally, for the amateur botanist, the subject lends itself admirably to the gentle pastime of water-colour painting. Edith Holden came of a long tradition going back over many generations (even Samuel Pepys arranged for his wife to have painting lessons, 'and I think she will do very fine things, and I shall take great delight in it'). Maybe a privileged minority used to be involved, but it was a pleasant and commendable and accepted practice that women should learn to paint and many attained very high standards. Happily in recent years it is a pastime that has not only been revived but has become more widespread than ever before—aided by easier transport in conjunction with all the many classes that exist in every town large and small.

A nature diary is a pleasure in itself; to be able to illustrate it not only redoubles that pleasure but makes the record even more valuable.

APRIL

The ground was carpeted with Anemones and Blue-bells, and here and there Primroses, and the tall, handsome plants of the Wood Spurge were very conspicuous with their red stalks and pale green flowers.

29

30

NOTES

Wood Anemone or Wind-flower
(Anemone membrosa)

MAY

Chaffinch's nest
and eggs.
Hawthorn blossom and Wild Hyacinths.

MAY

I saw a pair of White-throats today down Widney lane, they were evid=
=ently rivals, and were chasing each other through the bushes,
singing loudly all the time. By the Blythe I saw a very handsome
pair of Black-headed Buntings.

1

2

3

4

5

6

7

Red Campion
(Lychnis didrna)
Wild Hyacinth
(agraphis nutans)

Edith was always delighted to find a bird's nest, as she often shows by her notes and illustrations. A whitethroat's nest among the brambles—two hen blackbirds nesting quite close to each other—a robin with an uncharacteristic nesting-site beneath the roots of a tree—a water-hen on the stump of an alder (and it's interesting to mention that it has been claimed that a water-hen's first brood will sometimes help the mother make a nest for a subsequent family).

Edith's pleasure is understandable, for the bird's nest is one of nature's most charming artifices. The majority of birds build afresh each year; some like rooks, repair their old nests, some birds don't bother to make a nest at all. The peregrine falcon, that most majestic flyer, simply lays its eggs on some rock ledge or parapet. More extraordinary in this way are the hordes of sea-birds, such as razorbills and guillemots, which, nesting cheek by jowl, have no difficulty in returning to the right egg. And many ground-nesting birds lay their eggs in furrow or hollow, which would seem to pose a problem for their young. But in cases such as the lapwing, nature has overcome this vulnerability by first seeing to it that the eggs are highly camouflaged and second by the fact that the young lapwings are precocial, able to run about straightaway—though like many young creatures in danger they lie immobile in the hope of being missed by any predator.

Some birds make use of others' efforts—the sparrowhawk will often build on top of an old crow's nest or even a squirrel's drey. Puffins will make use of rabbit burrows, sometimes after evicting the rightful tenants. As for artificial aids, many centuries before we started to put up nesting-boxes for titmice and robins, the Lapps had taken advantage of the wild duck's penchant for nesting in hollow branches. They regularly erect nesting-boxes made of logs—and collect the eggs the ducks obligingly lay in them.

Some hard work is carried out by tunnel-nesters. The bill of the sand-martin is short and feeble-looking, yet the bird will persistently tunnel away at some convenient cliff or cutting, sometimes up to a foot or two. Charles Waterton (who died eight years before Edith was born) built a special bank on his Yorkshire estate to encourage sand-martins to nest there for the first time. As for the kingfisher, it will tunnel three or four feet, always upward for better drainage, into a riverbank, sometimes using a water-vole's tunnel as a starting

MAY

On my way back from Knowle this morning I made a halt at Widney.
I saw the Reed Buntings again by the Blythe, I think they must have their
nest there. There are quite a number of new flowers in bloom in the
marsh by the river, since I passed a fortnight ago.

8

9

10

11

12

13

14

Red Campion
(Lychnis diurna)
Wild Hyacinth
(agraphis nutans)

point. But of course the nests that chiefly evoke our wonder are the so-called 'cup' and 'domed' nests, most intricate of all. In many species both male and female take part in the work; in some cases, such as the lark family, it has been said that the male builds the outer nest while the female concentrates on the lining. And it is the female who will repeatedly shuffle round and round inside a nest, gradually fashioning by the pressure of her breast the soft but firm interior. Broadly speaking, the smaller birds, thrush, blackbird, chaffinch, robin, greenfinch and so on, are the most particular in their choice of materials. Others such as the ring-dove are more haphazard—it has even been known to use bits of wire for its nest which is often so flimsy the eggs can be seen from underneath.

'Domed' nests are the most elaborate. Alone among the crow family, the magpie builds a protective canopy over the main structure, a habit its cousin the high-nesting rook might well follow, as it sometimes has to spread its wings to protect its young from the sun. Some of the leaf-warblers, such as the willow-warbler, make 'domed' nests, but surely the most finely wrought and charming nest is made by the long-tailed tit. This exquisite, oval-shaped nest will take a pair of birds a fortnight to build, with such materials as wool, moss, lichen, even spider's silk and, of course, innumerable feathers: two thousand were recorded in one case. No wonder an old country name for the long-tailed tit was feather-poke. But poke-pudding, bottle-Tom, millithrums and mum-ruffin are also numbered among its soubriquets!

In that laboriously constructed home as many as a dozen fledgelings contrive to find space with their mother, a piece of overcrowding compounded at times by the male who will take refuge in the nest if the May nights turn chilly.

A bird that has no nesting problems is the cuckoo, a true bird of May, mentioned from time to time in *The Country Diary*. Carefree to a degree, it has intrigued us through the ages. As the nineteenth-century William Yarrell said in his *History of British Birds*, 'perhaps no bird has attracted so much attention, while of none have more idle tales been told.' On the one hand it has been looked upon as a harbinger of radiant times—Spenser's 'merry cuckoo, messenger of spring'—or the oft-quoted mediaeval 'sumer is icumen in, llude sing

MAY

Warm south west wind, with heavy fall of rain. Gathered some
wild Pear blossom and the first Cowslips I have picked this year.
Saw two hen Blackbirds sitting on their nests,—one in a hollow tree.
The Crab-apple is only in bud here yet, as are the Wild Hyacinths.
Heard the Cuckoo.

15

16

17

18

19

20

21

Red Campion
(Lychnis diurna)
Wild Hyacinth
(agraphis nutans)

cucu!' In contrast, Wordsworth spoke of 'the first cuckoo's melancholy cry', while for generations the cuckoo has represented marital betrayal. And even the Lapps (for the cuckoo voyages beyond the arctic circle) look upon it as a troll-bird, bird of the devil, an evil creature, and say that 'now the cuckoo has dunged upon the berries'—which are of great importance to them—'we shan't be able to eat them any more'.

As late as the eighteenth century, a naturalist as eminent as Carl Linnaeus declared that the cuckoo was a bird of prey—a nonsense his contemporary Gilbert White couldn't accept, any more than he could believe the assertion of the French anatomist, Monsieur Herissant, who tried to prove that the reason the cuckoo did not incubate its own eggs was because of 'the peculiar disposition of its bowels'. In true scientific fashion the curate of Selborne cut open a cuckoo in order to confound the Frenchman. Even a generation or two ago, gamekeepers often shot cuckoos because they believed they turned into sparrowhawks in winter, a superstition prompted by superficial resemblances in flight and the barred plumage.

The most favoured hosts for the reception of the cuckoo's egg are the meadow-pipit—whose fragile, trilling song Edith heard as the bird rose above the moors—the pied wagtail, dunnock, and at times the robin and the reed-warbler. The eggs vary in colour and often resemble to a surprising extent the eggs of the rightful parent. What is more, considering the ultimate size of the cuckoo fledgeling, the egg is comparatively small.

The cuckoo doesn't lay its egg in the host-nest. It lays it, probably, on the ground, afterwards carrying it in its beak to the chosen foster home—occasionally dropping it inadvertently on the way. And cunningly it waits until the favoured foster-parent has started to lay, knowing that otherwise suspicions would be aroused. All of a piece with the cuckoo's parasitical habits is the young cuckoo's ability—a violent impulse prompted by some nervous sensitivity in the hollow of its back—to get rid of the other eggs and even fledgelings in the foster-home.

And the voice of the cuckoo—Wordsworth's 'wandering voice'—E. W. Hendy's 'elfish wizardry'. Now here, now there, is it all part of the act? Birds will occasionally mob the cuckoo, instinctively knowing what it is up to: perhaps its elusive call is

MAY

I saw a Moorhen's nest today, it was placed on the stump of an old Alder tree, at the edge of a pond, just out of reach of the bank. The nest was built of sticks and pieces of dead reed and contained one egg.

22

23

24

25

26

27

28

Red Campion
(Lychnis diurna)
Wild Hyacinth
(agraphis nutans)

intended to mislead them as to its whereabouts, for as often as not the cuckoo calls on the wing? Both sexes call but the male calls more often. Does he do so to distract attention from the female, whose own less frequently heard call is a sort of explosive bubbling?

As for the great, fat, fluffed-up, greedy, insatiable young cuckoo which looks so gigantesque compared with its slim, astonishingly devoted foster-parent—how does it find its way to Africa a month, even two months, after the departure of its actual parents in August?

Nowadays many wildflower species have disappeared, torn up, indiscriminately gathered to extinction, chemicalized; hedges have been mutilated, banks bulldozed and pollinating insects sprayed out of existence. But in the days of *The Country Diary*, it was still possible to feel that with the coming of May especially, the earth had been born anew. A riot of colour and life is evoked by Edith's notes and one senses the pleasure she took in each fresh discovery. Fumitory, meadow saxifrage, black medick, (it's actually yellow!) the quaintly named weasel-snout, otherwise yellow archangel, lady's mantle, scorpion grass, wild garlic, blue field madder, pink clover and heart's ease, there's a never-ending catalogue of tiny floral gems. But all nature caught her eye, including the queen wasps she watched prospecting round the flowers of holly and rowan.

Most of us will remark on our sighting of the first wasp of the season, much more, say, than the first honey-bee. Perhaps it is basically because we are a little afraid of the wasp. She stings!—it is only the female wasp that stings, just as the worker bee, a female, stings, but the drone, a male, doesn't. But the wasp we are most familiar with only stings in self-defence. To kill her victim, maybe a fly, she uses her very strong mandibles, having first overpowered it with her strong legs.

There are several kinds of wasp, most of them solitary. The wasps that cause unease or even panic at tea on the lawn or at a picnic are social wasps which live in organized communities consisting of the queen and all her many daughters which do the work. The so-called oak-apple which Edith paints is caused by the grubs of the gall-wasp, a relation of which also causes the hairy swellings on rose-bushes. Another gall-wasp is responsible for the marble-gall in which its maggot lives; the pied woodpecker reputedly gathers these brown, hard little 'marbles' for the winter.

MAY

Saw some Dog Daisies in flower on the railway bank.
My sister brought home some beautiful White Meadow Saxifrage
she had picked in some fields near Hatton.

Common Earth Nut, Fumitory and Black Meddick in flower.

29

30

31

NOTES

Red Campion
(Lychnis diurna)
Wild Hyacinth
(agraphis nutans)

JUNE

Willow Warbler
feeding young.

JUNE

Cycled through Widnay. The Yellow Irises are out in the marsh there now, and at the edge of the stream I found the large blue Water For-get-me-not. While I was stooping to gather some, a beautiful Demoiselle Dragonfly came skimming across the water and lighted on a bunch of rushes.

1

2

3

4

5

6

7

Orange-tip Butterfly
(Euchloe Cardimines)

Purple Clover
(Trifolium pratense)

JUNE

Colour bursts forth even more radiantly in June and Edith's June is the essence of summer, her pages a continuing implicit praise of nature, as evocative as the notes of a piano coming from the twilit distance.

Frequently she mentions being near water in one form or another. By river or stream or marsh or pond or even ditch, she always found something to catch her interest. A sloping bank is crowded with figwort, whose dull dark purple flowers the bees enjoy, but which cattle won't touch perhaps because of the unpleasant scent coming from the trampled leaves. There's the stately yellow iris (than which surely only the water-lily is finer) which countryfolk sometimes call sedges or 'seggs', a word derived from the Anglo-Saxon for short sword, an allusion to the sharp, bold leaves that thrust up from the water. And over the stream, which sometimes washes it, caresses it almost, is the forget-me-not, among the most charming of wildflowers, with its clusters of tiny blossoms of a colour the ancient Chinese ceramic artists described as like 'the sky after rain'. One experiences though, a little shudder as Edith stoops down over the stream to gather some of the flowers, prefiguring as it does her tragic death fourteen years later.

And in the same water there is the golden, shining spearwort, which mediaeval beggars were said to use in order to produce artificial sores, and the bright blue brooklime, whose botanical name of *Veronica beccabunga* is rather like a beautiful girl being called Vanessa Snodgrass. Though it has to be admitted that after our earlier emphasis on the need for scientific names, that's perhaps a little inconsistent. But at the same time it could also be lamented that so many of the ancient country names for flowers have disappeared, such as deadmen's bells for the foxglove, cat-in-the-clover for bird's foot trefoil, lamb-in-a-pulpit for the wild arum and so on. If you asked a country child any of those names nowadays you would receive an uncomprehending stare.

Edith knew there was always life by the water, not only the wildflowers but birds such as the reed-bunting, which loves *any* water, from river to disused quarry, and will sally out repeatedly from a favourite perch to catch flies and moths. In some places, Cheshire for example, it used to be known as the water-sparrow because of its invariable habitat.

JUNE

I saw the Yellow Bitter Cress in flower in the marsh at Widney today.
Many of the meadows are golden with Buttercups, and some of the
fields are showing quite red, where the Sorrel is coming into flower.
Bright and sunny; the first summer's day we have had.

8

9

10

11

12

13

14

Orange-tip Butterfly
(Euchloë Cardimines)

Purple Clover
(Trifolium pratense)

And among the same osiers and bulrushes and loosestrife haunted by the reed-bunting and often by the reed-warbler and sedge-warbler (whose presence is made known by its garrulous, chattering song), the water-vole makes its unobtrusive way. This plump, chubby-faced, short-eared denizen of the river-banks is often maligned by being called the water-rat, suffering from the same spirit that classifies slow-worms as snakes and all snakes as dangerous. But the water-vole is no rat, and though it will dive for caddis-worms and water-snails on the river bed, it is principally a vegetarian. One of the most pleasant sights on the river-bank, the reward of patience and immobility, is of a water-vole plopping gently in and foraging for a suitably succulent stem, its favourite 'flote-grass' maybe, gnawing through it to bring it down, then, in characteristic pose, holding it in its forepaws to eat it, hunched in earnest concentration.

There are two much larger aquatic rodents Edith would not have been acquainted with, but which the present-day amateur naturalist could well encounter in certain parts of the country. Both were originally introduced to Britain half a century ago for fur-farming purposes. The inevitable escapes occurred and both species are now established feral animals. The first is the musk-rat (it's also a vole!), known in the trade as musquash; a chunky creature weighing a good two pounds. The second is the coypu, alias nutria, a bulky seven pounds or so. Both animals, particularly the latter, have done considerable damage to river-banks and dykes.

Another 'alien' that can all too often be seen in river-country in, for example, south-west England, is the mink, that larger and bloodthirsty relative of the stoat. It, too, was introduced because of its fur and, after innumerable escapes, it has become a prolific and successful species. Edith would be sad that it has largely replaced the otter, whose characteristic whistle could once be heard on the streams and rivers of Warwickshire, but which has now become rare.

Water, flowing or still, is one of the richest sources of wildlife, and no one fortunate enough to live near it will ever lack interest. Swallows, house-martins, wagtails, dippers, bats, fish, mammals, all use it in some way or another, either as a thoroughfare or a hunting-ground, largely because of the insect life that abounds in most stretches of water, insects and more microscopic creatures being the basis of so many food chains.

JUNE

Silver-weed, Wood Sanicle, Rough Hawk-bit, Small Hairy Willow-herb and Comfrey in blossom. The Wild Service-tree has been in flower for some weeks. This is the eleventh day of bright sunshine without rain.

15

16

17

18

19

20

21

Orange-tip Butterfly
(Euchloë Cardimines)

Purple Clover
(Trifolium pratense)

JUNE

On some rivers the most numerous of insects at times are the mayflies (still appearing on warm summer evenings long after the month for which they are named). They are the epitome of life's brevity, the name of their order, Ephemeroptera, meaning 'one-day wings'. In fact, of the forty or fifty species, some live only a few hours, others for two or three days at most.

In keeping with their brief existence they have a fragile beauty, their transparent wings criss-crossed with an intricate network of veining. More than any other creature, they conjure up an image of the trout-ringed pool, for fish rise eagerly to gulp them down as they perform their infinitesimal but urgent mating dance above the rippling water. Fishermen try sedulously to make artificial flies in imitation of the mayfly, but no skill or art can equal nature, especially in the case of the mayfly, whose existence usually stretches no farther than between the two twilights of dusk and dawn.

Daintily beautiful though the mayflies are, none of them, not even the Green drake, by far the largest, with a wing-span of two inches, is as striking as the various damselflies and dragonflies that Edith watched and painted, creatures redolent of high summer. She must have delighted in their exquisite, shimmering, metallic colours of emerald-green and vivid blue and fierce yellow and menacing red. The damselfly is handsome enough, but the larger dragonfly adds to *its* handsomeness a dramatic air of menace with its gig-lamp eyes and deliberate, spasmodic flight. Yet fearsome though it looks, it is quite harmless to humans, for it doesn't sting, in spite of its old country nickname of horse-stinger. But undoubtedly its appearance is formidable, to which is added its disconcerting ability to fly backwards!

Even though the dragonfly can't sting, it is a doughty hunter and will seize wasps and butterflies on the wing. Yet more voracious is its larva (the dragonfly doesn't go through a pupal stage). Hatched underwater, the so-called nymph is the terror of its neighbourhood, waiting in ambush for just anything that passes. It has extensible jaws that grip its prey like deadly pincers and in some of the larger species it remains in its underwater larval state for two or three years before the dramatic moment arrives for it to emerge and be transformed into one of the most spectacular of insects.

JUNE

Saw the first field of grass down, and cutting-machines at work in several clover-fields: Cow-Parsnip and Bird's-foot Trefoil in flower.

22

23

24

25

26

27

28

Orange-tip Butterfly
(Euchloë Cardamines)

Purple Clover
(Trifolium pratense)

As Edith knew, many other predatory insects exist in the water. One violent, carnivorous character is well named the water tiger: the dytiscus beetle alias the diver. Almost an inch and a half in length, oval in shape, dark olive-green bordered by yellow in colour, it prowls about many a pond preying on tadpoles, even young frogs and, it's claimed, fish-fry. It can fly well (not all beetles have the power of flight), and it will vary its beat according to food supply. It can often be seen rising to the surface of the water, where it pokes the end of its body out to renew its breathing supply by collecting bubbles of air under its wings.

Generally speaking, among the insects it is the butterflies—aerial gems such as the orange-tip and meadow brown and tortoiseshell and Red admiral and all the others featured in *The Country Diary* which are the best-known, being more apparent and superficially more attractive. But the world of insects in principle, though more difficult of access, as we might say, is well worth the trouble of studying, which can profitably be done in garden or field or park or even backyard.

The common rush, *Juncus conglomeratus*, which Edith illustrates, is an historic plant, affording a glimpse into social conditions in the days of our forefathers. For, suitably treated, rushes were for centuries the poor man's only source of light in the home. Let Gilbert White tell us about it, for his words cannot be improved upon.

> Decayed labourers, women, and children, make it their business to procure and prepare the rushes. As soon as they are cut they must be flung into water, and kept there; for otherwise they will dry and shrink, and the peel will not come away easily. After this they must lie out on the grass to be bleached, and take the dew for some nights, and afterwards be dried in the sun. Some address is required in dipping these rushes in the scalding fat or grease. The careful wife of an industrious labourer obtains all her fat for nothing; for she saves the scummings of her bacon-pot for this use. About six pounds of grease will dip a pound of rushes. If men that keep bees will mix a little wax with the grease, it will give it a consistency, and render it more cleanly, and make the rushes burn longer: mutton suet would have the same effect. A good rush has been known to burn for one hour and a quarter.

JUNE

Went for a long country walk through Catherine de Barnes, Hampton in Arden, Bickenhill and Elmdon. Everywhere the lanes were fragrant with Wild Roses, and Honeysuckle, and the breeze came to us over the hedges laden with the perfume of the Clover-fields and grass meadows. The grasses of

29

30

NOTES

Orange-tip Butterfly
(Euchloe Cardimines)

Purple Clover
(Trifolium pratense)

JULY

White Water Lily
(Nymphæa alba)
Great Dragonfly
(Ietinus pugnax)

JULY

In a corn-field of growing wheat, I saw a number of blossoms of the Opium Poppy. Their large red and purple blooms made fine patches of colour among the green blades. Had a beautiful white Water Lily given me from the pool at Packwood House.

1

2

3

4

5

6

7

Bee Orchis
(Ophrys apifera)

One small item is expressive of Edith's world, so different in so many ways from ours. Walking through a cornfield, across which meandered a footpath, she remarked that many stalks of wheat were entwined with bindweed or field convolvulus, whose delicately pink and white campanulate flowers respond so instantly to the sun, as if to affection. In a neighbouring field scarlet poppies slashed and streaked the up-thrusting blades with vivid patches. It was *Les Coquelicots* come to life indeed. (Edith was two years old when Monet painted that evocative scene.)

Edith would be unlikely to enjoy such scenes today, with crop-spraying helicopters patrolling the sky like baleful dragonflies and everywhere herbicides and insecticides pouring forth from the modern pandora's box of chemicals that we have opened. Nor would she recognize much of the landscape where thousands of miles of hedgerow and bank, some of them in existence since mediaeval times, have been bulldozed and pulverized in the name of efficiency. For in the generations that followed Edith's, mass production has overtaken agriculture and Goldsmith's dire prophecy that 'a bold peasantry, their country's pride, when once destroyed, can never be supplied' has indeed been fulfilled.

The quotations Edith was fond of using were always apposite. Here, alluding to July, the sixteenth-century Edmund Spenser's 'behind his backe a sithe, and by his belt he wore a sickle circling wide' was just as apropos as the 'sharp as a sickle is the edge of shade and shine' of George Meredith (still alive, an old man of seventy-eight, when *The Country Diary* was compiled). Both scythe and sickle were still very much in use for the hay-making Edith enjoyed watching, with the high-loaded wains swaying along between the rose-hung hedges, even though in farming in general, machinery was being increasingly used, horse-drawn reaping-machines and thrashing-machines, and traction-engines drawing the plough.

The farm tools and machinery Edith was familiar with, flail and winnowing-machine and wooden rake and, later still, even the tractor of pre-war days, are nowadays sought out eagerly, at great price sometimes, by a generation that hankers for a past which has suddenly become precious, just as the fragrance of some flower becomes evident after the passing heel has crushed it.

JULY

Went by train to Knowle and walked across the
fields to Packwood. Hay-making was going on in
most of the fields, but the grass was still uncut in the church meadows.

8

9

10

11

12

13

14

Bee Orchis
(Ophrys apifera)

Another accurate quotation is to the effect that a swarm of bees in July isn't worth a fly, in contrast with the far more valuable swarming in May and June, the reason being that the bees don't have so long now to establish themselves before winter. An earlier swarming is always a sign of a stronger hive.

Bees are of interest to the naturalist because of their importance in the ecology of a region. Where there are bees there are more flowers; more flowers, more insects and in turn more birds and other animal life. But bees are intensely interesting for their own sake, their marvellously organized communal life and their ability to transmute the nectar of flowers into a delicious, perfectly balanced food being among the wonders of nature.

As for their swarming, this is a necessary action to avoid the disaster of over-population. Normally a hive consists of about thirty thousand bees, but during the early summer this may rise to as many as eighty thousand. The young grubs are nursed with the utmost devotion, but the young queens will have been reared even more tenderly, being fed on royal jelly, a fluid produced in the heads of the bees. But it is always the old queen who leads the swarm, consisting of that part of the hive which will set up a new colony with her. Perhaps nature feels that her experience matters at such a crucial stage and that the young queen with her followers are best left in an already established home. (It was only in the seventeenth century that the Dutchman Jan Swammerdam, called 'the first real entomologist', established the existence of the queen bee. Until then, in Virgil's words, it had been thought that 'the kings lead forth the early swarms'.)

Sensibly, before take-off the departing bees gorge themselves on honey in order to sustain themselves until they settle in a new home. The hour of the swarm is fraught with intense excitement. The air is charged with what seems a menacing hum. In point of fact the bees are at their most docile when swarming; their only concern is to follow the queen and cluster locally about her. If the bee-keeper hasn't taken precautionary measures to secure the swarm, the bees, on their long stage in search of a suitable dwelling, will settle wherever the queen may from time to time rest, and the compact, single-minded mass is a strangely moving sight. Swarms have been known to settle in bizarre places—on the back of a donkey—on a

JULY

Cycled to Knowle, through Widney. The hedges are
a tangle of wild flowers now. There is a fine
show of wild roses, both the earlier Dog Roses and
the later white, trailing variety are in full bloom.

15

16

17

18

19

20

21

Bee Orchis
(Ophrys apifera)

railway engine stopping to take on water—even on a cyclist pedalling along a country lane.

Beloved of the honey-bee are the flowers of the lime or linden tree, which Edith paints. The lime is among the loveliest of trees, its blossom now in July filling the air with an almost dreamlike fragrance, its handsome branches eliciting a constant hymn of praise from myriads of insects. The honey from the lime is extremely pale, white almost, but of a delicious quality; and from the dried flowers country people used to make a pleasant infusion. In the seventeenth century Grinling Gibbons favoured the soft, smooth, pale yellow, even-grained wood of the lime for his superb carving.

The privet, too, which accompanies Edith's lime, also draws the bees and many other insects. It is usually thought of as a suburban hedge, but is a genuine country plant, growing in its natural state to six or seven feet. In the words of John Gerard, the Elizabethan herbalist, 'its flowers be white, sweet of smell, very little, growing in clusters, which being faded there succeed many clusters of berries, at the first greene, and when they be ripe, blacke, like a little cluster of grapes, which yeeld a purple juice'.

That purple juice was used for making a strong dye for woollen garments, while the berries themselves attract the bullfinch. But the privet mostly brings to mind the privet hawk-moth. The hawk-moths are the most magnificent in their particular sphere, from the strangely patterned death's head with a five-inch wing-span, to the beautiful bedstraw hawk-moth. Even the three-inch caterpillar of the privet hawk-moth is handsome, with its fine green colouring striped seven times with mauve and white. As for the moth itself, its splendid, mottled brown wings, sometimes tinged with a subtle pink, are set off by the boldly striped pink and brown of its substantial body.

No insect, but intriguingly like one, is the bee orchid featured in *The Country Diary*. Orchids usually conjure up a vision of the luxuriant, highly-prized blooms of hothouse or tropical jungle. But, on a more modest scale, some forty members of the orchid family grow wild in Britain, though some species are becoming all too rare. One of the family is this bee orchid, still to be found in parts of the country. At a glance the flower is quaintly suggestive of a bee, a form cunningly assumed by the flower to assure its own pollination. Male

JULY

I saw a beautiful kingfisher skim across the water
There were beds of tall rushes, nearly six feet high, with
blue green stems, and knotted clusters of brown flowers,
I think they must have been a species of Club Rush.

22

23

24

25

26

27

28

Bee Orchis
(Ophrys apifera)

bees clearly think so too and the scent of the bee orchid has been identified as being very similar to that of the female bee. Excited male bees are attracted to the bee orchid expecting to find mates and although they may be disappointed they do pollinate the flower. Other examples of mimicry are the protective mimicry of the stick insect, disguised as one of the twigs it lives on, or those of certain tropical spiders which mimic ants for hunting purposes.

Writing in the first century AD, Pliny the Elder said that the juice of the bee orchid was used for darkening women's eyebrows...

Across the pages of Edith's journal the kingfisher flashes, more common in those days than it is now. Perhaps our most brilliant bird, it suffered wretchedly in the past at the hands of the feather-trade at a time when women flaunted gaudy colours in their impossible hats. In addition, rod-fishermen were the bird's implacable enemy, not only because of its alleged depredations: 'I tried to get at that kingfisher', wrote Charles St John, that inveterate killer of wildlife, 'coveting the bright blue feathers on his back, which are extremely useful in fly-dressing.'

To have any chance of glimpsing this jewel-like bird, with its arrow-like flight and its ruddy chestnut and turquoise and subtle green which pass in a headlong blur, you must seek out a river or stream that provides it not only with good fishing, but whose banks afford scope for its tunnel-nest. The nest of the kingfisher is in stark contrast with the bird's breath-taking beauty: it consists of all the stinking remains of the small fish and tadpoles and other aquatic prey the parent kingfishers take to their several fledgelings.

JULY

It is the caterpillar of the Small Green Oak Moth (*Tortrix viridana*)
which ravages the Oak leaves.
Many of the Oak-trees which were so devastated by caterpillars
this year, are producing quite a new crop of foliage.

29

30

31

NOTES

Bee Orchis
(*Ophrys apifera*)

AUGUST

AUGUST

Went to Oban and back by West Highland railway; Quantities of
wild flowers all along the route, – on the banks, –Golden-rod,
Blue-bells and Heather, and in the bogs and marshlands –
Meadow-Sweet, Willow-herb, Trefoil and Knapweed

1

2

3

4

5

6

7

Heather or
(Calluna
vulga

The railways were at their height in Edith's day and, travelling as she did from time to time, she was always conscious of the wildlife that existed in the cuttings and on the embankments. Nowadays, with so many branch lines closed down and the permanent way—an ironic term!—ripped up, some of these forgotten highways along which the once-exciting iron horse used to gallop, have become miniature nature reserves. Badgers have at times found a place to dig their never-ending tunnels or roll at ease on a grassy ledge. Even when trains still steamed past, foxes often took up residence, passengers sometimes delighting in a glimpse of cubs on the steep slopes. Barn owls and kestrels have nested in the brickwork of ancient tunnels. Stonechats nest among the flourishing gorse, blackbirds and robins in the ruins of platelayers' huts. And the wildflowers especially star and spangle the long stretches of turf.

It's well worth while seeking out some of these derelict railway lines, which can be profitable hunting-grounds for the amateur naturalist. It is a strange, nostalgic experience to hike along some silent cutting that once upon a time carried an essential part of rural communication in a vanished and now regretted past.

It was by railway that Edith made her visit to Scotland, and it is interesting to note that less than sixty years before she wrote—indeed, only twenty years before she was born—Scotland, more especially the Highlands, was unknown territory to all but a few affluent English, such as the sportsman-naturalist Charles St John, who found it 'a perfect paradise, affording refuge to birds and beasts which had been exiled from richer lands, such as the wild cat and the marten, the sea-eagle and the osprey'. Although the works of Sir Walter Scott, notably *The Lady of the Lake*, contributed greatly to the increasing popularity of Scotland for tourists and sportsmen, up to the Crimean War period when the railway eventually linked London and Edinburgh, a laborious coach journey of several days was entailed. But by the time of *The Country Diary*, Scotland was a new, accessible land and it must have been an exciting prospect for Edith.

Here was entirely new wildlife for her, and the heather-clad hills over which the Golden eagle soared and on which the Red deer roamed must have seemed utterly different from the lush meadows

AUGUST

As I was walking across the fields to the Cattle today, a Snipe flew up from the grass at my feet, soon after I saw a Curlew alight in the field.

8

9

10

11

12

13

14

Heather or
(Calluna
vulga

and flowery lanes of Warwickshire. Nowadays the Golden eagle has revived a little from the bitter persecution it used to suffer at the hands of gamekeeper and shepherd and egg-collector, though its population is probably only a few hundred. In the air the Golden eagle is a magnificent sight, sailing majestically on its huge vans, watching from high up for hare or grouse or carrion sheep. On the ground, like so many of its relations, it moves awkwardly, almost waddling. As for the Red deer, it is our most imposing wild mammal, standing at times four and a half feet at the withers and weighing up to thirty stones. Its population in Scotland is the largest in Europe, its numbers on Exmoor and the Quantocks being moderate in comparison, while it is present occasionally in counties such as Derbyshire and Cumbria.

The Red deer stag in particular, with his imperious stance, his superb antlers (which can reach more than a yard in length and fifteen pounds in weight), and at times his headlong gallop when alarmed, is a thrilling sight, redolent of the splendour of nature. His antlers are among the most bizarre phenomena of the wild, as with all deer. Unlike the permanent horns of cattle or antelope, they are cast each year and grow afresh, strange branches becoming ever more splendid during the prime of the stag's life.

Watching deer is best carried out by the solitary individual or, occasionally, at the most two watchers in company, though even that can't really be recommended. Binoculars are essential; quiet clothing too, it goes without saying. The Red deer knows that Man's hand is all too often against him: hunted, stalked, slaughtered by poacher and crofter alike, the deer has many human enemies.

So it is a difficult and exasperating animal to watch. All too often you catch a glimpse of it vanishing over the skyline. Yet the deer *can* be approached if you are prepared to go to a great deal of trouble and discomfort, midges included. The best time for watching is very early morning and eventide. The best conditions are when there is no wind and enough cover. The deer's hearing is acute, but not as sharp as its other senses. Scent and sight are what it relies on chiefly, scent especially. And if there is any wind it is essential to approach the deer up-wind, even at the cost of making long detours.

But first find your deer! You must look long and hard, for the deer are often there without your realizing it, especially if they are at rest

AUGUST

Found three different species of Persicaria growing among the corn, and quantities of Hare-bells on the field-banks on the way home.

15

16

17

18

19

20

21

Heather or
Calluna
vulg

among the bracken, chewing the cud, the antlers of the stags barely
visible; hillmen say the growth of a stag's antlers keeps pace with that
of the bracken. And if you are keen-sighted, a cloud of insects may
make you aware of the deer's presence.

Edith's visit to Scotland illustrates how a holiday can enrich the
naturalist's experience, even in a short spell. The change of scene
sharpens the vision, contrasts present themselves and new
opportunities arise.

There was much to delight and interest her. How different from
the sedate pheasant of Midland game preserves would have seemed
the turkey-sized capercaillie, nicknamed in Gaelic 'horse of the
woods', whose caterwauling, explosive cries at times sound like a
chorus of banshees in the pinewoods. It is interesting, too, as an early
example of rehabilitation. Extinct in Britain by the 1780s, it was re-
established by the introduction of Swedish stock. Its smaller cousin
the glossily handsome black grouse, with its distinctive lyre-shaped
tail, is renowned for the springtime 'lek', when the blackcocks
display extravagantly in front of the admiring greyhens. 'In the midst
of the heather', wrote J. W. Fortescue in *The Story of a Red deer*
(1897), 'stood a number of greyhens, looking very sober and modest
and respectable, and round them, in a ring worn bare by the
trampling of their feet, a number of blackcocks were dancing like
mad creatures, with their beautiful plumage fluffed out and their
wings half spread, to show what handsome fellows they were.' In the
higher mountain tops there was that prototype bird of northern
solitudes, the ptarmigan, whose change of plumage to protective
white in winter gives it more chance to evade the marauding eagle
and the prowling fox. The ptarmigan is not the only highland
creature to change colour seasonally. The pelage of the 'blue' or
mountain hare turns white, while if temperatures are low enough the
stoat takes on its 'ermine' condition.

And of course there were the innumerable new or unfamiliar
flowers, the masses of golden rod mingling with the characteristic
harebells (the 'bluebells' of Scotland), the fragrant bog-myrtle, better
named sweet gale, the marsh-loving and pretty bog-bean and the
tiny, deep blue gentian. But of all this, of all the birds and animals

AUGUST

Found numbers of beautiful little purple Hearts-ease growing
on the short turf and came upon a big bog full of Grass
of. Parnassus, in the midst of the heather and Juniper
bushes. The berries of the latter are still green.

22

23

24

25

26

27

28

Heather or
(Calluna
vulga

and flowers, a plant that must have intrigued Edith almost more than anything was the sundew, one of the few insectivorous plants known in Britain, others being the bladderwort and the butterwort.

Insectivorous plants are an instance of nature's admirable balancing act. Most insectivorous plants exist in poor, boggy soil lacking the vital nitrogen to keep them flourishing. The solution is simple. They gain their nitrogen instead by eating insects. In the case of the sundew, its long-stemmed green leaves, patched with pinky red, are like long clubs. Round the edges grow hairy bristles or 'tentacles', the swollen ends of which are coated with a sticky substance. These blobs of 'sundew' glisten in the light and give the plant its name.

Along comes an insect and is attracted by the tempting sight, but, as Ben Jonson remarked, 'All is not sweet, all is not sound'. The insect lands on a leaf, gets stuck, and the tentacles close inexorably over it. Chemicals specially secreted let the plant digest its prey and when this is done, the leaf reverts to its former shape, ready for the next victim to be lured to its doom.

As for the butterwort, it takes its name from the glandular hairs on its leaves which produce a greasy, pale-yellow substance. Insects are caught in this, being then secured by the folding-over of the leaf edge. In contrast, the bladderwort, an aquatic plant, possesses traps in the shape of a number of hollow bladders on its submerged leaves. A trap is sprung when a water insect touches the trigger of sensitive hairs round the mouth of the bladder. This causes the bladder to open, water pours in dragging the victim with it and the trap closes immediately afterwards.

But first find your deer! You must look long and hard, for the deer are often there without your realizing it, especially if they are at rest among the bracken, chewing the cud, the antlers of the stags barely visible; hillmen say the growth of a stag's antlers keeps pace with that of the bracken. And if you are keen-sighted, a cloud of insects may make you aware of the deer's presence.

AUGUST

On the high ridge of hills between Aberfóil and the Trossachs I found the bright scarlet berries of the Bear-berry growing among the heather, and Sundew in flower. Found some Gentian beside Loch Vennachar.

29

30

31

NOTES

Heather or
(Calluna
vulga

September

House Sparrows
and
Oats.

SEPTEMBER

Rowed to the top of Loch Vennachar and pic-nicked
on the shore. The Brake Fern on the hills is be-
:ginning to turn bronze and yellow.

1

2

3

4

5

6

7

Fruit
of
Wild Guelder Rose
(Viburnum opulus)

SEPTEMBER

As the thistle is the national emblem of Scotland, it is only fitting that Edith should illustrate several of the family—there are many kinds. That Hibernian symbol often seems to be represented by a formalized version of the woolly thistle, with its great headpiece. In fact the Scottish thistle is what is termed the cotton thistle in *The Country Diary*.

Typifying the thistle's place in nature is the charming picture of a goldfinch feeding on the seeds of a plant, those seeds which, with the aid of their silky down, are spread far and wide on the wind, a highly effective method of dissemination. Bad farming, no doubt, but there is a certain reassurance about the presence of thistles. It implies the absence of ultra-commercialized, anaesthetizing, juggernaut agriculture—and is affirmed in the words, surprisingly perhaps, of Francois Rabelais, 'long live the thistles of the field', a sentiment echoed 350 years later by Gerard Manley Hopkins, 'long live the weeds and the wilderness yet'.

And it's a sentiment that would be echoed by much wildlife. Among birds, in addition to the brilliant goldfinch, you can often see linnets working sedulously on the thistle heads, occasionally uttering their pleasant, slightly plaintive *twee-ee, twee-ee*, as if expressing their satisfaction. In the goldfinch, the colouring of the sexes is virtually the same. In the linnet, the male is especially handsome, with his almost crimson breast and crown and forehead. On those northern moors Edith would have been more likely to see the twite, sometimes called the mountain linnet, a soberly clad little bird whose only splash of colour is the male's rosy pink rump. The twite enjoys the thistle equally and gathers at this time in considerable flocks.

As the diary shows, bumble-bees are constant devotees of the thistles, while on the sow-thistle, which strictly speaking is not a true thistle, in spite of its prickly leaves, there parade large numbers of those small beetles nicknamed soldiers and sailors because of their glossy uniforms, respectively reddish-brown and blue-black. The sow-thistle incidentally is so-called because its milky stems are said to be relished by pigs, but in mediaeval times the juice was recommended as a human medicine, 'beneficial to those that are short-winded and have a wheezing'.

Surely more closely associated than the thistle with the Highlands are the various heaths—Edith's ling and cross-leaved heath and the

SEPTEMBER

There was a curious, gold-brown dust lying all over the surface of the loch, which we thought must be Heather pollen, blown across from the hills.

8

9

10

11

12

13

14

Fruit
of
Wild Guelder Rose
(Viburnum opulus)

fine-leaved heath. And equally closely associated with the heather is the Red Grouse, that plump, chunky, handsome game-bird which is found only in Britain. Scotland is its main habitat, but its range stretches down into the Pennines and Wales, while it survives thinly on Dartmoor and Exmoor, where a few pairs were introduced in 1820 and again sixty years ago. Its fast, whirring, spasmodic flight and loud, assertive *go-back, go-back* are an essential feature of the bee-loud purple moorland. Though it will feed on crowberry and bilberry, its chief sustenance is the shoots, leaves and seeds of the ling. And if the winter snows are too deep, it will tunnel through them, seeking the buried heather tops.

All creatures have preferred feeding-sources, but some are more intimately associated with particular plants, as we saw with the privet hawk-moth. Among the most notorious are the so-called cabbage butterflies, the large and small Whites, whose caterpillars munch away at any available brassica. The pretty Purple hairstreak almost invariably frequents oak-trees, while the comma butterfly always used to be associated with hop-gardens. But the nettle is the favourite breeding ground of many species, such as tortoiseshell, peacock and Red admiral. A wild patch in the garden will produce its reward—and perhaps justify one's laziness.

One handsome insect linked very closely with one particular plant is the cinnabar moth, with its striking vermilion hind-wings and its dark brown, almost black forewings barred and spotted with crimson. It lays its eggs almost exclusively on the ragwort, which Edith illustrates. The plant's aliases of stammer-wort and stagger-wort refer to its alleged curative qualities for various ailments; but in Scotland it was nicknamed stinking willie because of its acrid odour when bruised, which repels rabbit and cattle alike, neither of which will touch it. The caterpillars of the cinnabar moth, protectively orange-yellow in colour and banded with purplish-black, emerge in great numbers at times, completely stripping the plants until nothing but the bare stems remain. But before that happens, 'St James's wort' is a handsome plant, worthy of John Clare's praise:

Ragwort thou humble flower with tattered leaves
I love to see thee come and litter gold
So bright and glaring that the very light
Of the rich sunshine doth to paleness turn
And seem but very shadows in thy sight.

SEPTEMBER

Walked to the Lake of Menteith and back across the hills. Unlike most of the scotch lochs the shores are flat and marshy and surrounded by large beds of reeds, which are a great resort of Water-fowl

15

16

17

18

19

20

21

Fruit
of
Wild Guelder Rose
(Viburnum opulus)

Moths are more usually associated with candlelight than sunshine, but confusingly the cinnabar moth prefers the bright day, a habit it shares with several other moths, such as the six-spotted burnet, whose bottle-green forewings are dotted with crimson spots. Normally, one way of distinguishing moths from butterflies is through their antennae. Those of the butterflies are clubbed, whereas in moths they are more varied, some being delicately 'feathered'. In the burnet, the antennae thicken in the middle before tapering towards the end. In general, too, the body of the moth tends to be more robust and hairy, unlike the slimmer, waisted body of the butterfly.

In *The Country Diary* the magpie moth is shown in close proximity with the ragwort. This isn't meant to suggest an association, for in fact, the magpie moth, one of the Geometer family, is most likely to be found on gooseberry or currant bushes or euonymus hedges. Its creamy-white background, marked with black and yellow spots is another instance of protective or warning colouring. Its larvae, like those of all the family, are known as stick or looper caterpillars. Geometer caterpillars are skilfully camouflaged by their mottled green or grey or brown colouring, in addition to which they are difficult to distinguish from the twigs they inhabit. As for their progression, this is influenced by the fact that they lack abdominal legs. So they have to make a purchase with their front legs, then arch or loop their bodies up in order to bring their hind legs forward, and then stretch along ground or branch while they take a fresh grip with the front legs again.

Some animals are more catholic in their taste than others; some concentrate with single-mindedness on one favourite source of food and may even die without it. Whenever you come across any creature, a note should be made of the habitat it was in and the plant it was feeding on or investigating.

An insect that isn't particularly fussy about its food-source, or rather that of its larvae, is the cranefly, popularly known as daddy-long-legs. The most common of the several hundred kinds that exist is *Tipula cleracea*, abroad in huge numbers in September, dancing and jerking, apparently aimlessly above lawn or field, but in fact looking

SEPTEMBER

Here were huge old Spanish Chesnut Trees, supposed to have been planted by the monks, and the largest Nut trees I have ever seen.

22

23

24

25

26

27

28

Fruit
of
Wild Guelder Rose
(Viburnum opulus)

for a suitable place to lay its eggs, its long, gawky legs allowing it to straddle the grass. In a fortnight's time the eggs will hatch out into the egregious 'leather-jackets'—so-named because of their tough skins—which will proceed to anger many a gardener because of the damage they do.

Edith mentions the great number of pike in one of the lochs and the stuffed specimens in their glass cases lining the walls of her inn-parlour. But others of the tribe no doubt found their way on to the inn dining-table, for as the seventeenth-century fisherman Robert Nobbes put it, 'September or October are the chiefest months for the goodness of the pike—which grows too fast to be fat and is delicious and most grateful to the Palate.'

However, it's usually the pike that does the eating while still in its native lake or river. Its character is summed up by its nickname of river-wolf, for it is truly ferocious. One oft-related but authentic example of its rapacity is of an eight-pound specimen which seized a salmon of its own size. A violent conflict ensued, but the salmon, for all its desperate struggles, was unable to shake off its attacker. After two hours of this watery drama, the salmon was exhausted, whereupon the pike proceeded to swallow it head first. It took the pike three days to absorb its victim and for a week afterwards it lay swollen and sluggish in the river, unresponsive even when prodded by a stick.

But that was a small pike! Weights of fifty pounds, lengths of four or five feet, have often been recorded. One pike caught in Loch Ken was estimated at seventy-two pounds. Nothing is safe from the pike, including its own kind, for it is a confirmed cannibal, while waterfowl, wild duck, frogs, voles, all are potential prey. Shadow green in colour, its long jaws expressive of its nature, it lies patiently among the reeds as still as a sunken log, waiting for the moment to swirl out through the water and drag down its victim, like some freshwater shark.

SEPTEMBER

Goodbye to Scotland and back to the Midlands once more.

Scarcely any of the foliage on the trees is turned colour.

29

30

NOTES

Fruit
of
Wild Guelder Rose
(Viburnum opulus)

October

Yellow-Hammers
feeding in stubble.

OCTOBER

I was shown some wonderfully fine specimens of the Parasol Fungus today, pale fawn, flecked and shaded with darker tones of the same colour.

1

2

3

4

5

6

7

Yew
Taxus baccata

I t isn't surprising that Edith was so fond of the yew. No tree is more historic, not even the oak. In mediaeval times it was the yew, planted compulsorily in churchyards, that provided the long bow which was the chief reason for England's military superiority over the French in those brutal, interminable wars cloaked by time in a false romance.

Apart from that, the yew is a magnificent tree, with its spreading canopy of almost horizontal branches, its massive, many-columned, iron-red trunk, and its beautiful pink-red berries, beloved of thrushes and blackbirds, which discard the poisonous stones, more sensible than cattle which sometimes browse off its equally poisonous foliage.

The yew trees Edith mentioned so often were at Packwood, that charming manor, sixteenth-century in origin, standing in the Forest of Arden, scene of *As You Like It* and now National Trust property.

Chestnut, beech, oak, all of whose fruit Edith paints, were also historic trees, each in its way playing a part in the national and rural economy of the past. True, the timber of the horse chestnut is worthless, but it has two claims to fame, its place in the age-old schoolyard game of conkers, and its glorious springtime candelabra, unrivalled for their beauty. As for the sweet or Spanish chestnut (possibly introduced by the Romans, along with fallow deer and pheasant), when sound, its timber is almost as good as that of the oak, but too often it suffers from ring-shake disease and becomes foxy-hearted.

Its principle use was in making hop poles and fencing stakes. The wood for such purposes is produced by the very ancient practice of coppicing, carried out by allowing the shoots from the stump of a felled tree to continue growing in the form of long, straight, sturdy single branches which are cut back every several years. As for the fruits of the tree, they conjure up visions of chestnut-roasting by the fire (or *marrons glacés*!). But in the days when there were far more trees, the chestnut was used extensively by country people, for it grinds into a useful 'flour'.

Apart from human use, the sweet chestnut was of great value in rural areas for free-ranging pigs which fattened admirably on the nuts, just as they did on beech-mast and acorns. In regions such as the New Forest, pannage was an ancient and jealously guarded right of the commoner. It meant more to him than the fact that the oak-tree,

OCTOBER

Walking through the fields today to Elmdon Park, I saw numbers of the little blue blossoms of the Field Speedwell, these, and Mayweed, Pink Campion and a few belated Blackberry blossoms were the only wild flowers I saw.

8

9

10

11

12

13

14

Yew
Taxus baccata

for example, was of such importance for England's traditional wooden walls.

It wasn't only humans who benefited from these trees! Because of their particular fruit, oak, beech and chestnut are of immense value to many kinds of wildlife. Jays, ring-doves, nuthatches, pheasants, squirrels, dormice, wood-mice, bank-voles, badgers, deer (and, once upon a time, wild boar) all enjoy those various fruits. Innumerable insects, crustaceans and spiders, pursue their minute but dramatic lives among the bark and foliage. Pupae of butterfly and moth pass their strange dormancy in crack and crevice, before emerging as utterly different creatures from the caterpillars that once nibbled the leaves. Fungi and parasitic ferns establish themselves on the branches. The often hollow trunks of sweet chestnuts provide fox or owl with a lodging.

The summer's sun is stately, overpowering at times, disturbing even. In autumn (perhaps in St Luke's 'little' summer) its warmth is more benign, for a brief moment there is an air of well-being, of a dreamlike permanence, though one knows only too well this will not endure. Red admirals and peacocks paint the still air with their colours; tardy hummingbird hawk-moths worship at the Michaelmas daisies, their wings a blur of astonishing energy; in the fields gossamer spiders will soon spread their fairylike parachutes and take off on their migration.

The season's cornucopia is spilling out. Nature pours forth her many riches with prodigal generosity. And autumn 'shadowless like Silence, listening to silence', is evoked in all its mellow fruitfulness by *The Country Diary*. Some of the gleaming fruits all too quickly spoil. The devil has surely spat on the blackberries, as country people say, but the sloes, with their marvellous blue powdery bloom, will not be at their best until the first frosts have cut their bitterness a little. Sloe gin is one of those nice rationalisations sometimes indulged in, gin by itself being considered not quite genteel, whereas the purple juice released from the well-pricked berries transmute it into something respectable. But even that handsome colour doesn't match the beautiful translucent pale amber of crab-apple jelly.

However, in spite of all the preserves and concoctions that find their way into many a store-cupboard, most of these autumn fruits

OCTOBER

I brought home some of the fruit of the Wild Service tree and some Acorns, to paint. Looked for Crab Apples, but could not find any, although the was a quantity of blossom in the spring. Probably they have all been gathered.

15

16

17

18

19

20

21

Yew
Taxus baccata

are quite properly for the benefit of the wild creatures. Even the hedgehog will accept a well-ripened crab-apple windfall, though in spite of Pliny and others he doesn't carry away the fruit on his spines. Bluebottles, wasps and half a hundred other insects feast on the overripe blackberries, which blackbirds enjoy, too, judging by their droppings. And they and the mistle-thrushes gulp down the richly decorative rowan-berries, although the song-thrush isn't quite as keen.

Keep watch on most wild fruit-bearing trees or bushes and you will find some activity going on.

One tree, or bush, that has always held a place in country affections is the hazel. Its pliant branches were often used for making sheep-hurdles, but it was the nutting that mattered, when 'gathering the ripe, clustering bunches brown' was the traditional occasion for a rustic Sunday afternoon outing along the lanes and through the spinneys. Under the nut trees now you will begin to find the earth strewn with empty shells, and this may well be the only evidence you will get of the dormouse's presence. For this tiny, furry rodent is almost exclusively nocturnal. But it is one of our prettiest mammals, with its pale tawny, sometimes reddish pelt, its long bushy tail, and its huge eyes. Its method of dealing with the nuts is as neat as the nuts themselves. With its sharp incisors it bores a hole as precisely as if with a gimlet, before extracting the kernel with the tip of its tongue.

The dormouse has every reason to profit from such rich autumn feeding and it will eat hawthorn peggles as well, for example. It is the only British mammal to hibernate in the strictest sense of the word, sleeping far more profoundly and for a longer period than the hedgehog. During its long winter sleep it will lose well over one third of its weight. A hard winter suits the dormouse best; a mild season may cause it to wake up when food is still scarce.

Contrary to popular belief, the squirrel does not hibernate, though it may not be so active in winter. It too appreciates the hazel-nut (and the sweet chestnut and beech-mast) and will make little caches of food, often forgetting these subsequently. It will also eat certain mushrooms or toadstools, including the fly agaric that Edith paints. This handsome and poisonous *Amanita muscaria* that glistens in the

OCTOBER

The Swifts have all disappeared and for some days I have not seen any Martins flying about.

There are still some Swallows to be seen, but the greater number have gone south.

22

23

24

25

26

27

28

Yew
Taxus baccata

autumn sun is almost the prototype of the toadstool associated in popular imagination with gnomes and elves; however, as it happens, the majority of British fungi are edible, though few have any real culinary value, except for the familiar field mushroom, the delightful primrose-yellow chanterelle and various boletuses and others, including the springtime morel. One 'toadstool' that Edith mentions is eminently eatable, though it needs a lot of butter in the cooking. This is the parasol mushroom whose arrival usually heralds the first frosts.

Earlier on, Edith had noticed large numbers of house-martins gathering on the roofs in preparation for their departure. These regular late summer or early autumn congregations of martins and swallows are a stirring sight, but one tinged with regret—and renewed wonder that these summer visitors can find their way unerringly over thousands of miles. But all the sibilant twittering that goes on while these close-packed flocks gather on telephone cable or barn ridge is not just pointless excited avian talk. All those staging posts are for the purpose of refuelling. At each stop the birds take the opportunity of feeding on the abundant insects, while even as they rest, idly so it seems, they are storing up solar energy to give themselves strength for the arduous, dangerous flight southward.

We more consciously welcome spring and summer visitors, partly because they herald more clement times, partly because with longer days and finer weather there is more opportunity for us to enjoy them. But now that those welcome visitors are departing—or, like cuckoo and swift, have long since departed—others are arriving out of the far north. Indeed, on the same day as Edith records the last chiff-chaff, she mentions redwings and fieldfares coming in from Scandinavia. The redwing is a nocturnal migrant and sometimes its soft flight call can be heard high overhead, even in towns. Ironically, though these superbly beautiful thrushes come to spend the winter with us, other members of the family leave us; many mistle-thrushes winter in North Africa and many song-thrushes fly off to the soft climate of southern Ireland.

But perhaps the full drama of bird migration is best experienced down on the sea-shore and the estuaries which begin now to ring with an incomparable wild music.

OCTOBER

The last of our summer visitants has taken his departure;
About a fortnight ago a Chiff-chaff was constantly to be
seen hopping about the Gooseberry bushes in the garden; —
the last to leave us, he is usually the first to arrive .

29

30

31

NOTES

Yew
Taxus baccata

November

Starling
(sternus vulgaris)

NOVEMBER

The wife of a game-keeper living next door to the cottage where I was painting the birds, showed me two fine, stuffed specimens of Night-jars, which her husband had shot in the neighbourhood.

1

2

3

4

5

6

7

Nipple-wort

Edith mentions seeing two nightjars—in November! A record worthy of a letter to *The Times*? Could it be that these summer migrants from Africa (sometimes they come from as far as the Cape) had lingered on because of a plentitude of moths and beetles on the mellow air? Alas, no. They were stuffed specimens, having been shot by a local gamekeeper (one of that breed who shoot first and ask questions afterwards, or rather say nothing about it, especially in the case of a protected species).

Because of a superficial resemblance of some predatory birds in its long-tailed, long-winged, shadowy hawklike flight, the nightjar used to suffer from a similar prejudice among game-preservers as the cuckoo did. Could it be that gamekeepers suspected the combed or pectinated claw the bird possesses? Nobody seems to have divined the real use of this claw, though Gilbert White reported having watched a nightjar 'more than once, put out its short leg while on the wing, and, by a bend of the head, deliver something into its mouth. If it takes any part of its prey with its foot, as I have now the greatest reason to suppose it does with these cockchafers, I no longer wonder at the use of its middle toe, which is curiously furnished with a serrated claw.'

However that may be, and intensely interesting as it is, the nightjar's customary method of hunting is by means of its beak. This is extremely short, but has a very wide gap, and in the case of sizeable insects it will open its mouth to its full extent to catch them. Its broad beak is thickly beset by comparatively long bristles which may be designed to help in catching its food. The lovely crepuscular flight of the nightjar, when it comes and goes, sweeps and glides silently as a moth, is in contrast with its almost squatly reptilian appearance on the ground or as it lies lengthwise on some branch. It is surely one of the most perfectly camouflaged of birds. Brindled with various dead-leafy, brackeny, shades of brown and grey, the nesting female is to all intents and purposes invisible as she broods her creamy-white eggs mottled with brown and purple on a non-existent nest among the woodland debris. With her eyes closed to mere slits, she will sit tight until almost trodden on, when she rises like a shadow, often not even with a croak of alarm.

Country people, to whom in the past the coming of twilight was an uneasy time, have always suspected the nightjar and their attitude

NOVEMBER

Went for an early morning walk across the fields to Elmdon Lane
to make some sketches of a Blackbird and Thrush at a
cottage there. It was a grey, perfectly still morning with
a slight fog, that veiled the distant woods and trees

8

9

10

11

12

13

14

Nipple-wort

to it is characterized in the many nicknames the bird was given. Flying toad alluded to its appearance; fern-owl to its habitat. Goatsucker derived from its habit of flying round cattle in search of insects and the implication of that name was on a par with the slander that hedgehogs used to suck the teats of cows. Lych (meaning corpse) fowl summed up the dread of any night creature—especially one with such nerve-racking silent flight.

But Jenny-spinner was the nicest of these appellations. It referred to the characteristic, gentle, churring, whirring, trilling song of the nightjar that vibrates on the evening air. It is a sound redolent of magical evenings in May and June, delicately scented with the ineffable fragrance of bracken, the heavier sweetness of the hawthorn, when the badger's striped head wavers out from his sett and the doe reassuringly nuzzles her fawn, when glow-worms light the heathland track and the nightingale utters its throbbing crescendo.

All this imagery is evoked at the threshold of winter because of those dead, faded birds proudly mounted in their glass case.

Edith remarks that she had been unaware of nightjars occurring in Warwickshire, though she had often seen them on Surrey commons and on Dartmoor. To begin with they are very unobstrusive birds, your best chance of seeing them being at twilight, that always dramatic and profitable time of day. In addition the 'puckeridge' is very local in its habitat, nowadays probably its greatest numbers being found in the New Forest area and parts of East Anglia.

One bird Edith often saw in her neighbouring woods was the green woodpecker, gorgeous in its greenish-grey underparts, its brilliantly vivid mantle, striking yellow almost golden rump and scarlet crest. Its undulating flight is confidently easy for a comparatively large bird, 'rising and falling rhythmically', it has been said, 'as though it were a swimmer breathing invisible breakers'. Its ringing, laughing cry is a joyous sound of the English countryside—in spite of its supposed ability to call up rain, which gives rise to one of its many names: rainbird. Probably no other bird has been accorded so many country nicknames, among them yaffle, popinjay, sprite, woodspite, yuckel, yaffingale, nickerpecker and many others.

The woodpecker is admirably adapted and structured for its

NOVEMBER

Stormy day with a gale of wind and rain from the West. I walked home from Solihull in the afternoon All the way along, the leaves were whirling down from the trees in hundreds and dancing along the road before me.

15

16

17

18

19

20

21

Nipple-wort

arboreal life, with its straight, sharp, powerful bill, its 'climbing feet' in which two toes face forwards and two backwards, enabling it to move with great agility up or round the trunk of a tree, while its short stiff tail acts as a supporting brace when it is hammering away in its constant search for the myriad insects that inhabit the bark.

But the most remarkable feature of the green woodpecker is its tongue. This is exceedingly long and can probe deep into otherwise inaccessible crevices and chinks and fissures. Indeed, the length of this appendage is shown by the fact that its roots are coiled up at the back of the head. In addition, the tip of the tongue is very sticky so that the bird can pick up ants, for which it has a particular passion, with devastating speed. But its diet is wide-ranging, embracing anything from woodlice to acorns.

Woodpeckers in general have sometimes been accused of damaging trees by their incessant hammering, but they are interested chiefly in wood already rotten, which is where most of their prey lives. Even the nesting tree may look sound from the outside but is almost certainly decaying inside the trunk. The woodpecker makes a horizontal entrance which is then extended downwards for about a foot, the nest consisting simply of the resulting chips of wood. The young are notoriously noisy and you often hear them grumbling away in a discontented undertone.

The greater spotted or pied woodpecker, being extremely shy, is often thought to be less common than it is. W. H. Hudson called it not only our most handsome woodpecker, but our most beautiful bird, with its superbly polished plumage of black and white and crimson. The loud, vibrating rattle sometimes heard in springtime is made by this woodpecker, for the yaffle doesn't drum nearly as much or as emphatically.

Thomas Hood, contemporary of Wordsworth and Coleridge, once wrote

No shade, no shine, no butterflies, no bees,
No fruits, no flowers, no leaves, no birds—November!

A libel, of course, and one easily refuted. For the drama and interest of nature never falters, even if sometimes it has to be looked for more

NOVEMBER

The sun had a most remarkable appearance just
before setting tonight. I never saw it look so large
in my life. It was deep crimson, shaded with purple
which gave it a globular appearance.

22

_____

23

_____

24

_____

25

_____

26

_____

27

_____

28

_____

Nipple-wort

thoroughly and in unexpected places. One superbly dramatic activity takes place in November, with the running of the salmon, though many of these magnificent fish wait until the early months of the year.

The whole life cycle of the salmon is fraught with danger, from the time the eggs are laid. Not even all the twenty thousand eggs an average female salmon lays are fertilized; many are simply washed away. Of those fertilized, eels devour huge numbers. Even the dipper will take them.

In the two or three years the young salmon takes to grow from alevin to parr and from parr to smolt, it is constantly in danger from heron and pike and mink and poacher, not the old-fashioned folk-hero, but a double-dyed villain armed with monofilament nets and explosives and poison, collapsible boats and fast cars. And of course there's the additional modern hazard of pollution, often caused by careless or unscrupulous farmers.

And then, surviving all this, when the salmon smolt makes its way to the deep waters south of Greenland, its main pelagic feeding ground, it is beset by other dangers, from seals to avaricious fishermen using illegal small meshes. A year or more of rich ocean feeding and the now full-grown grilse feels urgently, irresistibly impelled to return to its native river to perpetuate the species. Its ability to find the waters of its birth is still one of the mysteries of nature, but may well lie in its sense of smell.

What is unquestionable, however, is the strength of the salmon's inherent determination to return home. Nature must be obeyed; life everlasting, whatever the difficulties and hazards. Nothing will stop the salmon and it is appropriate that the Romans should have dubbed it Salar, the leaper, for, where it is not provided with 'ladders' to ease its progress, it will leap ten or eleven feet to overcome weir or waterfall as it makes its way towards the far-distant spawning grounds or redds, the waters of which, ironically, may be too shallow even to cover the backs of the mating fish.

It is worth going many miles for the chance of seeing the returning salmon leaping defiantly, persistently, their glorious, iridescent, silvery, muscular bodies, epitomizing nature's determination to survive. 'Though you drive Nature out with a pitchfork', wrote Horace two thousand years ago, 'she will find her way back.'

NOVEMBER

Cycled to Solihull, and back through the lanes past the
Oak woods, The sun was shining brightly, lighting
up the dying fronds of Bracken among the under-growth,
and the scanty foliage on the half bare Oak trees.

29

30

NOTES

Nipple-wort

DECEMBER

DECEMBER

Very bright and clear with a cold wind from the north east.
For many weeks past the birds have been coming to be
fed in the mornings. Today I put out a cocoa-nut,—to the
great joy of the tom-tits

1

2

3

4

5

6

7

Holly (Ilex aquifolium)

DECEMBER

'In December keep yourself warm, and sleep', is the advice in one of the quotations in *The Country Diary*. That's all very well for the likes of dormice and hedgehogs, the bees, butterflies and innumerable insects, the lizards, amphibians and snakes that nature equips to withstand the rigours of 'Winter, ruler of th'inverted year'. But, apart from the migrants who flee south as if from a plague, the birds are not so fortunate, in spite of the ancient belief (held until two hundred years ago!) that some, such as swallows, hibernated in the mud or the reed-beds.

As suggested in the notes for February, vital help can be given to many birds by means of bird-table and bird-bath. The cold and the snow are great levellers. Jay, magpie, seagull, jackdaw, carrion crow, woodpecker, greenfinch and pied wagtail will all gratefully accept your offerings—and, typical of nature's opportunism, predators such as kestrel and sparrowhawk will sometimes realize what is going on and lurk about to ambush finch, sparrow and blackbird.

Nevertheless, altogether it is only a minority of birds that can benefit from human largesse, some never venturing near a bird-table, while some species are more susceptible to the winter than others, being less adaptable in their food-range. The kingfisher (which Edith so often saw) is hard hit by a severe winter, when it is deprived of its food-supply by the streams freezing over. In desperate times it is forced to fly long distances down to the sea-shore to try its luck. But that is of little avail if the shore line freezes too far for it to find shallow enough waters to prospect.

Ironically, although the redwing comes to us for the winter from Lapland and Norway, it is less able to withstand the severe cold than is its more robust fellow-traveller, the fieldfare. Some of the redwing's diet consists of berries—and for a time there are still many of these around, such as ivy, holly, privet and hawthorn. But the redwing is rather like the song-thrush in preferring insects and worms. By the time the weather has made these too scarce, most of the berries have been stripped by mistle-thrush and fieldfare and blackbird. One sure sign of an approaching storm is a sudden descent of a flock of redwings, usually the shyest of birds, on to garden bushes such as *Cotoneaster frigidus* to gorge themselves on any remaining berries in desperation before fleeing farther westward.

One rarer berry, deeply interesting historically and botanically, is

DECEMBER

Hard white frost and fog. This is the first real winter's day we have had. Crowds of birds came to be fed this morning. There were great battles among the Tits over the cocoa-nut.

8

9

10

11

12

13

14

Holly (Ilex aquifolium)

the mistletoe, featured in the last painting of all in *The Country Diary*. Innumerable legends and beliefs surround it. In the prose *Edda* the story is told of how the beautiful and worthy Baldur, son of the great god Odin, protected against all other dangers, was yet killed by an arrow tipped with mistletoe (thanks to the mischief-making Loki). But we associate it chiefly with the Druids, to whom it was the Golden Bough, symbol of fertility; this is perhaps, the origin of the rite of kissing beneath mistletoe at Christmas.

The mistletoe is semi-parasitic, its seeds implanted in the bark of its favourite hosts, apple and poplar and hawthorn—for ironically it doesn't particularly favour the oak with which traditionally it was so closely linked. This happens when birds, especially the significantly named mistle-thrush, clean the sticky liquid of the berries from their beaks, wiping them to and fro on the bark. The resulting growth sends out a sucker into the sapwood of the tree, from which it obtains nourishment in the form of water and mineral salts. The water, carried to the pale green, evergreen leaves, which by now have sprouted, is transmuted with carbon dioxide by solar energy into sugars and starch, the plant's food.

Perhaps the bird most adversely affected by severe cold is the wren. That natty, neat, nimble, stumpytailed, explosively-voiced bullet of a bird, shown by Edith in characteristic pose, has an interesting history. Originally a native of North America, it gradually, many thousand years ago, began to move westwards into Siberia and eventually into Europe and Britain. It is one of our smallest birds, having received the ultimate accolade of being featured on the farthing, our smallest coin until the 1960s. It is also, surprisingly, our commonest bird (that's not the same as most numerous).

But its population suffers seriously during a hard winter when its usual food of insects and spiders simply vanishes. Normally the wren is a very solitary character with its own strictly defined territory. However, circumstances alter cases, and as the old country saw has it, 'when jenny-wrens cluster, then there'll be a bluster!' The 'feathered mouse' or 'mouse's brother', to use two of its many aliases, realizes that there is at least warmth if not safety in numbers. Instinctively wrens gather together in the cold at roosting-time. Sometimes they

DECEMBER

We woke up to a storm of whirling snowflakes this morning, — the first snow this winter. The storm was soon over however and it was followed by bright sunshine and a sharp frost at night.

15

16

17

18

19

20

21

Holly (Ilex aquifolium)

make use of the beautiful nests they made in the previous spring. As many as seven wrens have been found huddling together in one of them. But with increasingly dire weather they gather in such numbers that they need more room. One winter, thirty wrens were found roosting in a thatched roof, piled on top of each other, the whole feathery mass heaving gently as the wrens breathed.

But the tally goes on. Thirty-one were counted going to roost in a nesting-box only six inches square—not much bigger than a tea-caddy. The unbeatable record, surely, is forty-six wrens in another nesting-box. Bitter indeed must have been the cold that night to drive those tiny birds together in such great numbers. Next day several of them were found dead on the frozen ground underneath.

Wren
(Sylvia troglodytes)

It is not only the birds for whom winter is a difficult time. During the autumn months the badger would have been sedulously cleaning out its sett, removing stale bedding and carting in bundles of fresh bracken and grass, clutching them to his belly, and shuffling in

DECEMBER

After a rapid thaw and four days of wonderfully mild, still weather, without wind or rain, the wind has gone round to the east and it looks as if we might have a frosty Christmas after all.

22

23

24

25

26

27

28

Holly (Ilex aquifolium)

backwards. For the badger, fairly populous in Edith's Warwickshire, is the cleanest of wild creatures and also the most house-proud, his sleeping-quarters far snugger and more hygienic than the slum the fox lives in. But although the badger takes such pains over his winter comfort, he does not hibernate, at least in this country.

The fact is that the badger had waxed fat during the preceding months, reaching an average weight of twenty-seven pounds in the male, while one of forty-three pounds was once recorded. So to a certain extent the animal can live on its fat and is always lighter when spring comes round. The notion that the badger hibernates is disproved, if by nothing else, by the coming of snow: for his tracks are frequently visible, even his dung-pits are still used, incontrovertible evidence that he is active, albeit to a lesser extent.

The badger sensibly dislikes dirty weather, not merely snow, and is quite capable of lying up for two or three nights in succession before hunger urges him out into the long winter night. Indeed, it is just as well those winter nights are so long, for the badger has to cover many miles to obtain food now that there are no young rabbits or juicy bulbs or wasps' nests and even the earthworms have gone underground.

The fox, too, has a hard time of it in the kind of December recorded in *The Country Diary* when all Britain lay under snow from John o' Groats to Land's End. But, by the end of the month it is more than food that concerns the fox. It is the mating season, a matter of supreme urgency whatever the weather—gem-hard stars stringing their necklaces across the sky while the earth is shrouded in snow. One of the most dramatic sounds of the winter night is the eerie, gasping scream of the vixen, a stark cry out of the mysterious depths of nature, somehow inducing an atavistic shiver and transporting us back through countless ages to the days when our distant ancestors huddled round their cave fire and harkened with foreboding to the voices of the wild.

Ironically, that nerve-racking mating-scream and the answering bark can, in these days of the urban fox, be heard on many a town common or municipal park while the lights of the twentieth century flash on all sides.

DECEMBER

The frost still holds, snow lightly throughout the day.
The birds have become wonderfully bold this last week
since their usual hunting grounds have been buried
in snow.

29

30

31

NOTES

Holly (Ilex aquifolium)